VICTOR MOLLO'S
BRIDGE CLUB

How to
Turn
Masterful
Plays
into
Monstrous
Points

BY
VICTOR MOLLO

FOREWORD BY
RICHARD L. FREY

A Fireside Book
Published by Simon & Schuster, Inc.
New York

Formerly titled *Masters and Monsters*

Copyright © 1979 by Victor Mollo
All rights reserved
including the right of reproduction
in whole or in part in any form.
First Fireside Edition, 1987
Published by Simon & Schuster, Inc.
Simon & Schuster Building
Rockefeller Center
1230 Avenue of the Americas
New York, NY 10020
Originally published in Great Britain
by Faber & Faber Ltd as *Masters and Monsters*
FIRESIDE and colophon are registered trademarks
of Simon & Schuster, Inc.

Manufactured in the United States of America

1   3   5   7   9   10   8   6   4   2 Pbk.

Library of Congress Cataloging in Publication Data

Mollo, Victor.
Victor Mollo's bridge club.

Reprint. Originally published: London; Boston: Faber and Faber, 1979.
"A Fireside book."
1. Contract bridge.   2. Contract bridge—Anecdotes, facetiae,
satire, etc.   I. Title.
[GV1282.3.M578   1987]   795.41'5   87-13545
ISBN 0-671-64237-5 Pbk.

CONTENTS

ACKNOWLEDGMENTS

The Menagerie was conceived in the early sixties in the columns of *Bridge Magazine*. Most of the adventures recounted in these pages go back to those early days and have not appeared in print elsewhere. Some of the more recent exploits of the Griffins have been described in New York's *Bridge World* and in California's *Popular Bridge*. And month by month they are recorded in the ACBL *Bulletin*, in America, and in *Bridge Magazine*, now *Bridge International*, in England. I thank the editors for the warm welcome they always extend to the heroes and villains of my Menagerie.

But my greatest debt of all is to the Griffins themselves, who have taught me so much by their deplorable lapses, no less than by their savant coups and dazzling masterstrokes.

The everyday mechanics of bridge can be learned through books. Technique on the higher plane is too closely bound up with the human element to be mastered away from the table. That is why I owe so much to the Griffins—because they are so very, very human in all they do and say, and above all, in the way they play.

I can only hope that the reader will find them as entertaining and as instructive as I have done, and as I still do, for I meet them every day.

FOREWORD

It's not often you can promise a bridge player, "You'll have fun with this book." But I am ready to do so. And if you have never before read one of the books about Victor Mollo's bridge menagerie, I *guarantee* you will enjoy this one.

While you are chuckling over the foibles of the animals who people Mollo's zoo and recognizing in them many of the human characteristics of your own bridge companions, you may learn something about the importance of table presence and psychology as well as the technique of playing the fascinating collection of deals the author has gathered to illustrate the virtuosity of the Griffins' genius, Hideous Hog. But the purpose of this book is to entertain the reader; education is purely incidental, and you will see for yourself why Mollo enjoys the reputation of being the author of the funniest books on the game.

Like most humorists, Victor is, in person, a very serious man. His twenty-six non-zoo books are sprightly and so is his conversation, but you may wonder where he conceals the font of wit that flows so effortlessly from his pen. His great good fortune is that he would rather play bridge than do anything else, except perhaps write about it.

He is almost exclusively a rubber player. He plays for stakes, not for overtricks which slow up the game and curtail the advantage of getting to play the most possible rubbers. He is impatient with those who play for what he calls "Monster Points," and before he devoted so much time to writing he was considered one of the most consistent money winners in the British empire (perhaps he still is). But he is certainly the most prolific bridge writer—his books and articles have been translated into French, German, Dutch, Swedish, Danish, Norwegian, Spanish and, a rare distinction, into Greek and Hebrew!

Foreword

A few personal notes: Unlike most authors, Victor doesn't type. That chore is attended to by his wife, the Squirrel (if she has another name, I don't recall hearing it), who doesn't play bridge! His calligraphy is as beautiful as his English. I revel in the correspondence we have maintained for many years. His vocabulary is immense, his diction flawless and his writing bears not the faintest trace of "accent," although in fact he was born in Russia!

But why am I trying to introduce Mollo the man when you are ready to enjoy Mollo the author? If this is the first of his four "menagerie" books you are reading, I know you will want to find the other three as soon as possible, and you will be glad to learn that a fifth is already in the hands of his publishers.

—Richard L. Frey

INTRODUCTIONS

Are you a Griffin?

You probably are, though you may be unaware of it, so here's a simple test.

Is bridge a medium through which you like to express yourself? Do the cards, leaving the humdrum world behind, take you to a plane where you can be bold and brilliant, resolute and resourceful, clever, calculating and cunning?

Does playing well bring you a glow of satisfaction? Does playing badly make you squirm?

Yes? Then, of course, you are at heart a Griffin. The members of the exclusive club which you are about to join, differ from lesser mortals only in being more colourful, more vibrant, more clearly defined in all their traits, good and bad. They have the same frailties, commit the same follies and are just as comic in their vanity and their pretensions as the rest of the human race.

The situations in which they find themselves are often dramatic and sometimes absurd, but though the colours have been heightened, all are taken from real life.

Unlike the paper battles of distant champions, known to us only by their names, the duels of the Griffins bring us close-ups of characters whom we have often met and can readily recognise. And as we follow every thrust and parry we know that they are not just seeking to win money or matchpoints, but above all, in so doing to boost their egos.

It is the human element, bringing with it spice, pathos and excitement, which allows us to savour to the full every coup—and every lapse from grace.

Have you been to our club before? Perhaps you've visited *Bridge in the Menagerie*, or maybe you've played with the Griffins in *Bridge in the Fourth Dimension*. If not, let me take you behind the scenes and introduce you to our leading members.

H.H.

Much the best player and the biggest bully is H.H., aptly named the Hideous Hog. Regarded as a genius, he cannot understand why he is so grossly underrated. His greatest rival is

Papa

Papa the Greek, who alone among the Griffins challenges his supremacy. A fine technician, intuitive, so subtle is Papa that he can false-card with a singleton. And he always knows what everyone will do—except that the Hog usually does something else.

Karapet

The Greek's best friend is Karapet Djoulikyan, the Free Armenian, without doubt the unluckiest mortal since Job. He expects the worst and is rarely disappointed. Worse still, no Griffin these days will listen to his hard-luck stories, and one or two have even had the temerity to tell him their own.

R.R.

As lucky as Karapet is unlucky is the Rueful Rabbit. Gentle, generous, always ready to help—more especially his opponents—the Rabbit used to think of himself as the second-worst player in the world. But that was before he met the Toucan.

R.R. rarely knows what he is doing or why he is doing it, but hovering over him is the best Guardian Angel in the business, and every time R.R. drops a clanger the Angel waves his magic wand and the ugly duckling turns into a bird of Paradise.

T.T.

Timothy the Toucan, a comparative newcomer, owes his nickname to a long, red nose and a disconcerting trick of bouncing in his chair. Longing for affection, the Toucan tries to ingratiate himself with one and all by admitting every mistake before he makes it. Technically, he is in the same class as R.R and W.W.

W.W.

Walter the Walrus, a retired accountant since early youth, is our outstanding exponent of the Milton Work Count. Brought up on points and percentages, he espouses in bridge the philosophy of Molière's doctors, firmly believing that it is more honourable to land in the wrong contract with adequate values than to reach the right one without them. What points are to the Walrus the rules and regulations are to S.B.

S.B.

The Emeritus Professor of Bio-Sophistry, commonly known as the Secretary Bird, knows the laws backwards and would sooner invoke them against himself than not invoke them at all. Opponents dislike him. Partners fear him. Nobody loves the Secretary Bird.

C.C.

Colin the Corgi, a facetious young man from Oxbridge, bites and snaps and rarely troubles to hide his contempt for lesser players. Still lacking in experience, he has all the makings of a future master.

Ch. Ch.

Charlie the Chimp is our newest member. An inveterate chatterbox, he is interested in every hand, except the one that he is playing, and likes the inquest on every deal to continue through the next one. This greatly confuses the Rabbit, but then so does everything else.

O.O.

Oscar the Owl is the most respected figure at the Griffins. Our Senior Kibitzer, he is a stern disciplinarian and demands the highest standards in manners and decorum. As Chairman of our Monster Points and Ethics Committees, he insists that no partner, not even the Toucan, should be abused or vilified until the hand is over. And he frowns on all sharp practice, even when there's no other way to make or break a contract.

P.P.

Peregrine the Penguin is Oscar's opposite number at the Unicorn, where the Griffins play duplicate on Thursdays. Precise and somewhat pompous, the Penguin is a committeeman, as well as an accomplished kibitzer, and helps us to award Monster Points.

And now, having met the stars, you will know what to expect when you watch them perform.

Chapter 1

MONSTER POINTS

"Master Points!" scoffed the Hideous Hog. "Why, the whole idea is cockeyed."

H.H. was not in a good mood. His doctor had told him to lose a stone—or rather not to put on another—and he was dieting rigorously. No refreshments between tea and dinner, foie gras on weekdays only, and no carbohydrates except bread and potatoes. Unaccustomed to privations, the Hog was taking a jaundiced view of life.

"Why cockeyed?" enquired Oscar the Owl, Senior Kibitzer at the Griffins.

"Because," snapped the Hog, "if you reward success, you should punish failure. The two go together."

"Are you suggesting . . .?" began the Owl.

"Certainly I am," replied the Hog warmly. "If you present Master Points for merit, you should inflict Monster Points for demerit. I have nothing against virtue, as such, but why should sin go unpunished? Minor peccadilloes don't come into it," went on H.H. "Anyone can be careless and miss some baby smother play or common trump squeeze. For that sort of thing a black mark or two would suffice. It's the enormities that call for special treatment."

"But some enormities are more enormous than others," objected O.O. "Where would you draw the line? And who would do it?"

Thoughtfully the Hog sipped my sherry. Having consumed his ration—his Spartan diet allowed two drinks only before dinner—he had ordered the barman to remove his glass. After a while he resumed: "Anyone would be entitled to submit a claim. Should it be contested, a panel of experts would arbitrate. We'll have a Monster Points Committee with the Owl, the Penguin and yourself. And in due course we'll have Master

Monsters and Life Monsters, just as they do with Master Points."

That's how the Monster Points idea was born. It was largely inspired by the début of Timothy the Toucan, a new member who owed his nickname to a large, polished rubicund nose and to a habit of bouncing in his chair as if he were on the point of hopping over to another. Smooth, sleek and shiny, draped in a suit of midnight blue, with a satin tie of burnt orange, Timothy's colour scheme blended perfectly with his unusual personality.

It took us some time to get used to his curious habits at the card table. Instead of gloating, moaning, reviling partners and jeering at opponents, as do ordinary players, he oozed an unnatural humility from every overworked pore.

"How kind of you, partner, to explain so patiently where I went wrong," he had told the Hog after being subjected to a flood of abuse.

"Sorry," he said to Papa the first time they played together, "of course, I should have realised your singleton was top of nothing. I am afraid I am not really with it today."

And on cutting Walter the Walrus for the third time in succession, he greeted him with: "Splendid! I've got my favourite partner." The startled Walrus thought for a moment that there were only the two of them there to make up the four.

The Rabbit was delighted to find someone at last who would play with him all his cherished conventions.

"I haven't quite mastered Monaco . . ." began R.R.

"The strong notrump?" broke in the Toucan, on a more mundane plane.

"By all means," agreed the Rabbit.

"We'll keep to 16–18. Astro in defence, Baron responses over 2 NT, Flint, Jacoby transfers and Roman Blackwood, or would you prefer the Culbertson 4–5? I like both myself," added R.R.

"Then let's play both," agreed Timothy, who never said 'No'.

"Ace from ace-king?"

"Certainly."

The Elegant Way

Such had been the preliminaries when the Rueful Rabbit cut
Timothy the Toucan against Papa the Greek and Walter the
Walrus. These were the North-South hands on the first deal:

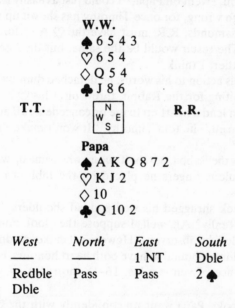

W.W.
♠ 6 5 4 3
♡ 6 5 4
◇ Q 5 4
♣ J 8 6

T.T.

R.R.

Papa
♠ A K Q 8 7 2
♡ K J 2
◇ 10
♣ Q 10 2

West	North	East	South
——	——	1 NT	Dble
Redble	Pass	Pass	2 ♠
Dble			

The Toucan opened the ◇ A. Then, seeing his partner's three,
he switched to the ♣ 4. The Rabbit won the trick with his king,
cashed the ♣ A and exited with the three. The Greek, who had
thrown his ♣ Q under the ace, took the trick with the jack in
dummy and continued with a small diamond, which he ruffed in
his hand, with the ♠ 8, carefully preserving the deuce.

When both opponents followed to the first round of trumps,
Papa put down his hand with a characteristic flourish. "I won't
waste your time," he announced. "There are several ways of
making sure of the contract, but we can make assurance doubly
sure and we can do it, what's more, the elegant way."

After drawing the remaining trump, the Greek overtook his

♠ 2 with dummy's ♠ 3 and proceeded to explain exactly what he would do.

"I will play the ◇ Q, discarding the ♡ 2 from my hand. Since you lead ace from ace-king, Timothy is marked with the ◇ K and whatever he returns will present me with my eighth trick.

"Mind you," went on Papa, "I could just as easily lead a heart. I couldn't go wrong, for once Timothy has shown up with seven points in diamonds, R.R. must have the ♡ A Q for his 16–18 notrump. The result would be the same, but the loser-on-loser play is prettier, I think."

Suiting his action to his words, he detached dummy's ◇ Q, and without waiting for the Rabbit, threw on it his ♡ 2.

"You can lead a heart up to me or concede a ruff and discard. Please yourself," he told Timothy. "It won't make the slightest difference."

But it was the Rabbit, not the Toucan, who came up with the ◇ K. With tremulous fingers he placed on the table a nondescript heart.

The Greek shrugged his well padded shoulders. "Ace from ace-king? Really? Ah, well, I suppose they look much alike to some people," he observed. "However, it makes no difference. If R.R. is no longer bound to have both heart honours, he must still have the ace. Even so his 16–18 notrump is the barest minimum."

As he spoke Papa went up confidently with the ♡ K. Diffidently Timothy took it with the ace. The Rabbit's ♡ Q won the sixth decisive trick for the defence. This was the deal:

W.W.
♠ 6 5 4 3
♡ 6 5 4
◇ Q 5 4
♣ J 8 6

T.T.
♠ 9
♡ A 9 8
◇ A 9 8 7 6
♣ 9 7 5 4

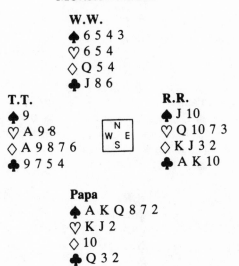

R.R.
♠ J 10
♡ Q 10 7 3
◇ K J 3 2
♣ A K 10

Papa
♠ A K Q 8 7 2
♡ K J 2
◇ 10
♣ Q 3 2

"I am frightfully sorry," said T.T. to the Greek, who was spluttering with indignation. "I know that we agreed to lead the ace from ace-king and though it's no excuse, of course, I just didn't have the king. I promise it won't happen again."

"No, no, it's all my fault," the Rabbit hastened to comfort him. "I forgot for a moment all about the strong notrump. We all play the weak one here, you see, and we nearly doubled them into game through it all, dear oh dear."

"The elegant way!" seethed the Walrus.

"People shouldn't be allowed to use conventions they don't understand. It's not fair to opponents," fumed Papa.

The Fourteenth Trick

To cut short the recriminations, the Rabbit dealt again quickly and opened 2 ♣.

For the sake of convenience he is shown as South in the diagram.

T.T.
♠ A J
♡ 2
♢ K 10 2
♣ 8 7 6 5 4 3 2

Papa
♠ Q 5 4 3 2
♡ —
♢ J 8 7 6 5
♣ A K Q

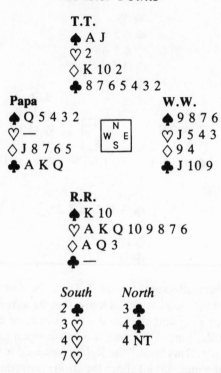

W.W.
♠ 9 8 7 6
♡ J 5 4 3
♢ 9 4
♣ J 10 9

R.R.
♠ K 10
♡ A K Q 10 9 8 7 6
♢ A Q 3
♣ —

South	North
2 ♣	3 ♣
3 ♡	4 ♣
4 ♡	4 NT
7 ♡	

In the post-mortem Timothy accepted full responsibilty. He wasn't absolutely certain what he meant by his 4 NT, but he admitted frankly that he wasn't *au fait* with Roman Blackwood. He promised to look it up that same night and meanwhile tendered his abject apologies.

The Rabbit, taking 4 NT as Culbertson, could identify in partner's hand either three aces, or else two aces and the king of a bid suit. It was all he needed to bid a confident 7 ♡.

The Greek doubled gleefully. It was clear to him that something had gone wrong with the ace-showing apparatus and the distribution promised to be unkind. In pleasurable anticipation he led the ♣ A.

The Rabbit ruffed. Then he rearranged dummy so that the trumps should be on the right, called for coffee and chocolate-almond biscuits, apologised for keeping the table waiting and methodically counted his tricks.

On his score pad he jotted down: 2 plus 7 plus 3 plus 0 equals 12. He had forgotten the first trick and needed, therefore, one more, a fourteenth, for his grand slam. How could he get it?

The only hope was to set up a club. This, however, required a lot of entries in dummy and only two were visible to the naked eye. The Rabbit had seen H.H. take some amazing finesses to create entries and as he led out a couple of rounds of trumps, just to clear the air, he resolved to emulate the master.

On the hearts Papa shed two small diamonds, but the Rabbit's mind was far away and he noticed nothing unusual.

To the fourth trick R.R. played the ♠ 10, finessed against the queen, and ruffed a club. Then came the ◇ 3 and a breathtaking finesse against Papa's jack. Another club ruff was followed by the ◇ Q, which the Rabbit overtook with the king in dummy.

Were the clubs good? R.R. could not be sure, but since he seemed to have an entry to spare, he ruffed another club before entering dummy once more by overtaking his ♠ K with the ace. The three-card position was:

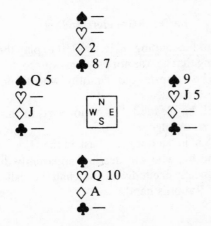

On the ♣ 8, the Walrus, panting noisily, threw his last spade. The Rabbit thought of ruffing it, since he had no losers, but having taken so much trouble to set up that club he was not going to be done out of it. So he discarded his ◇ A—if only because it looked spectacular—and led dummy's other club. Walter's trump came as a shock, but somehow it didn't seem to matter. He was home.

"Beautifully played," said the Toucan, who had never seen anyone make fourteen tricks before.

"You gave it to him," jeered the Hideous Hog, who had strolled in during the hand.

"Of course I could have stopped him by going up with the ♠ Q or with the jack of diamonds for that matter," cried the Greek in anguish, "but do you expect me to guess that he is going to fluke his way into a quadruple Grand Coup?"

"No, no," agreed the Hog. "Of course not. But you shouldn't have been so careless, throwing diamonds on hearts. Our friend would have spotted a black card at once, and had he known that he needed to shorten his trumps four times he could never have done it. After all, he is only dangerous when he doesn't know what he is doing. You could have told him, and you missed the chance."

Perfect Misunderstanding

Through a misunderstanding, R.R. was left to play the next hand in 1 ♠. Forgetting that he was not playing Monaco, he made what was intended to be a transfer bid. Timothy, who did not recognise it, accepted the blame.

"Forgive me," he pleaded. "I am not used to this high-class game. You are so indulgent."

"How many 'os' in 'smoodger'?" asked the Hideous Hog in a loud aside. Timothy, who was dealing, apparently did not hear him. After bouncing excitedly in his chair he called 2 NT. I looked into the Rabbit's hand.

♠ 2
♡ Q 7 6 5 4 3 2
◇ 9 8
♣ Q J 10

The auction was brisk and brutal. R.R. bid 3 ◇. The Toucan raised him to 6 ◇ and Papa doubled exultantly. He guessed what had happened and it gave him considerable pleasure to dot the 'is' and cross the 'ts' for the benefit of the luckless Toucan and for the amusement of the kibitzers.

"Your partner's 3 ◇," he purred softly, "is artificial. It is the Flint convention, and requires you to bid 3 ♡ automatically. Partner passes or alternatively bids 3 ♠, if that is his suit, and you, in turn, pass. This allows the contract to be kept to the three level on a weak hand and it ensures that the lead should run up to the strong hand. And what could have been better than that when you are thirty up?"

The Rabbit was looking embarrassed. The Toucan was visibly distressed.

"You see," cooed the Greek, "your partner may not have a diamond at all, not even a small one." As he spoke, he led a spade.

Dealer North—N/S Game and 30

T.T.
♠ A 4 3
♡ A 8
◇ A K Q J 7
♣ A 3 2

Papa
♠ 10 9 8 7 6 5
♡ K J 10
◇ —
♣ K 9 8 7

W.W.
♠ K Q J
♡ 9
◇ 10 6 5 4 3 2
♣ 6 5 4

R.R.
♠ 2
♡ Q 7 6 5 4 3 2
◇ 9 8
♣ Q J 10

South	West	North	East
—	—	2 NT	Pass
3 ◇	Pass	6 ◇	Pass
Pass	Dble		

Taut and tense, the Rabbit went up with dummy's ace and ruffed a spade. The ♣ Q followed, and then the ♣ J. Both held. The third club took him to dummy and allowed him to ruff another spade with his remaining trump. Next came a heart to the ace and three rounds of trumps. When Papa showed out, the Rabbit shook his head ruefully. The Walrus had more trumps than dummy, and there was a heart to lose as well. It didn't seem to matter which of the three remaining cards he played next, but the ♡ 8 was nearest his thumb, so he flicked it to the centre of the table.

With nothing but trumps left, the Walrus was compelled to ruff and to lead a trump from his 10 6 into dummy's J 7.

The Rabbit didn't like to say anything, but he felt sure that the defence had slipped up badly.

"Curious hand," observed Oscar the Owl, "despite a 6-0 trump break, a slam is possible only in diamonds."

"So long as it is played the wrong way round," pointed out Peregrine the Penguin. "If Timothy is declarer, Walter can upset the applecart by opening a trump."

"Why did you double, Papa?" asked the Walrus. "You only had seven points."

"Because you had six trumps, and I knew it on the bidding," replied the Greek. "Surely you didn't expect me to let them off?"

The Walrus felt sure that there was a flaw in the argument, but for the moment he could not spot it.

"I have been meaning to ask you," said the Rabbit to the Toucan: "shall we play McKenney or Lavinthal?"

Chapter 2

LAW AND ORDER IN THE MENAGERIE

"What a pity," said Oscar the Owl, our Senior Kibitzer, "that so gifted a man should be so taken up with the Laws."

"True," agreed Peregrine the Penguin, O.O.'s opposite number at the Unicorn, "yet it's hardly surprising, for it's much the best part of his game."

We were discussing the Emeritus Professor of Bio-Sophistry, known to us as the Secretary Bird on account of his appearance and his curious habit of hissing when provoked—that is, most of the time.

A serious legal imbroglio had held up the game for twenty minutes or more earlier that afternoon. The Rueful Rabbit, who had cut the highest card, chose the winning seats and the blue cards. Timothy the Toucan, his partner, wanted the reds. "They won the last two rubbers," he explained.

"Very well," agreed the Rabbit amiably, "we'll have the reds."

"Too late," objected S.B.: "you have already exercised your privilege." Easygoing and good-natured, R.R. and T.T. gave in at once. Not so a master kibitzer, who argued that since the blue pack had not been cut for the deal, there was no firm commitment.

"Tcha!" scoffed the Walrus, S.B.'s partner. "They've got the winning line which is what counts, of course. How can the colour of the cards matter? Sheer superstition. Tcha!"

But the Emeritus Professor had been roused and there was a dangerous gleam in his pince-nez. The wild tufts of hair, standing out at right angles to his ears, bristled with wrath and his Adam's apple, surmounting a rich brocade tie of bilious yellow, throbbed angrily as he joined battle.

With two junior kibitzers rallying to S.B. and a player who was dummy at the next table coming in strongly on the other side, argument and counterargument flashed furiously to and fro.

"All this silly quibbling in my time," fumed the Hideous Hog, who was waiting to cut in. "Frittering away my money at £5 a hundred!"

Eventually, someone brought a brown-and-yellow pack from another table and an honourable compromise was reached. But by then it was too late for the Walrus, who had a train to catch, to finish, or rather to start, the rubber. Tempers were badly frayed when the Hog took his place and drew the Emeritus Professor as his partner.

Dealer South—Love All

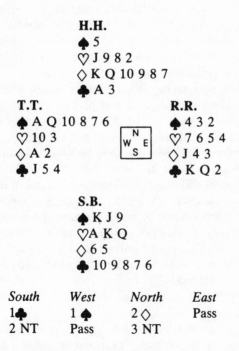

H.H.
♠ 5
♡ J 9 8 2
◇ K Q 10 9 8 7
♣ A 3

T.T.
♠ A Q 10 8 7 6
♡ 10 3
◇ A 2
♣ J 5 4

R.R.
♠ 4 3 2
♡ 7 6 5 4
◇ J 4 3
♣ K Q 2

S.B.
♠ K J 9
♡ A K Q
◇ 6 5
♣ 10 9 8 7 6

South	West	North	East
1♣	1♠	2◇	Pass
2 NT	Pass	3 NT	

The auction followed a natural course.

"Wants to play every hand," growled the Hideous Hog, but since there was nothing he could do about it, he sullenly raised S.B. to 3 NT and resigned himself to the unaccustomed role of dummy.

Looking more than ever like a Toucan, with his long, red nose standing out against the background of a shiny, black alpaca jacket, Timothy carefully selected the ♠ 8. He knew little about the rule of eleven and thought vaguely that it had something to do with the Mafia. But he had been taught that it was unbecoming, if not downright immoral, not to lead the fourth highest of his longest suit and he was rarely at fault in matters of etiquette.

Winning the first trick with the ♠ 9, the Secretary Bird led a diamond to dummy's king, then a heart to the ace. As he did so, he pressed together his thin, bloodless lips, and meditated. The contract hinged on those diamonds and either defender might have the ace or the jack or both. If the Rabbit was holding up the ace, the future was bleak. If the Toucan had started with the ◇ A J xx, it was little better—unless he finessed the ten. Before leading a second diamond, S.B. played off his hearts.

The Rabbit was paying little attention. Bored with his dreary cards, he sighed and fidgeted and played with his pencil. His mind wandered. What had he done with that letter to the Tax people? He remembered distinctly not posting it, but where could he have put it? Mechanically he followed suit. Twice he played before his turn, and each time the Professor remonstrated. When he did it again, on the third round of hearts, S.B. turned on him angrily. "I warned you twice. Since, however, you find it too much trouble to wait your turn, I am compelled to invoke the rules. If you will be good enough to turn to page 31 of the International Laws of Contract Bridge, you will find under subsection (c) of section 57 the penalty prescribed for a premature play by a defender."

The Toucan bounced unsteadily. The Rabbit tittered anxiously.

"If I am correct in presuming that you have no heart," went on S.B., turning to the Toucan, "I request you play a diamond."

The Hog, strangely silent till then, had been peering into T.T.'s cards. Now he weighed in vehemently on the side of his opponents.

"Surely, partner," he cried in shocked tones, "you are not going to take advantage of a trifling, an insignificant peccadillo. Be generous. Our friend's little, er, procedural error has done you no harm, no harm at all. . . ."

"In accordance with the Laws," persisted S.B. implacably, "I specify the diamond suit. Kindly play a diamond."

With a woebegone expression, Timothy the Toucan produced his only remaining diamond, the ace.

The Hog snarled in impotent rage, for the contract, unbeatable before, was now doomed. With the ♢ A out of the way, the Rabbit's jack became a certain entry, and it was only a matter of seconds before a deadly spade pierced S.B.'s gizzard. In the name of the Laws the Professor had encompassed his own destruction.

"I congratulate you, declarer, on your brilliant defence," said the Hog bitterly. "Superb piece of unblocking!"

"Sorry, Timothy," apologised the Rueful Rabbit. "I'll try to concentrate."

An Unusual Defence

The next two deals were uneventful. Then, after three passes, the Hog opened 4 ♠. "Fourth hand," he told us later, "is the ideal position for pre-empting. Not only does it shut out partner, who might otherwise bid notrumps or show his suit, but it also makes it difficult for opponents to come in. If they chance it, partner should have enough to beat them, so you can usually double in comfort."

All passed.

For the sake of convenience the diagram is turned to make H.H. South.

S.B.
♠ 7 5
♡ Q 3
◇ 8 5 4
♣ K Q J 8 7 6

R.R. 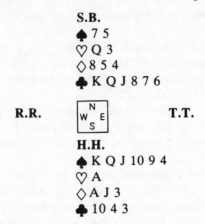 **T.T.**

H.H.
♠ K Q J 10 9 4
♡ A
◇ A J 3
♣ 10 4 3

The Rabbit opened the ♣ A and followed with the five, which the Toucan ruffed. Coming in with the ♡ A, the Hog led the king of trumps, and when the Toucan produced the ace, he sat back and grunted contentedly, for the contract was now safe.

With a sigh, the Toucan gathered the trick and subsided miserably in his seat.

"Oh dear, oh dear," he lamented. "I am frightfully sorry, but I've found a little club." With a guilty look he produced the deuce.

"A revoke," snapped S.B. "The deuce of clubs," he continued, "becomes a penalty card and must be played at the first opportunity. Two tricks will be transferred . . ."

"Certainly not," cried the Hideous Hog, thumping the table. "I wouldn't dream of allowing, I mean enforcing, a preposterous penalty for a trivial slip. Please, my dear Timothy, pick up that first trick and substitute . . ."

A loud noise, not unlike a low-pitched whistle, drowned the rest of the sentence. "You have certain duties to your partner," hissed S.B., "and waiving penalties at his expense is not one of them. The Laws are quite explicit. Page 33, section 63 . . ."

"I will not have a revoke!" roared the Hog.

"Kindly desist, both of you." The Rabbit spoke with quiet dignity. "We appreciate your magnanimous gesture, H.H., but we seek no favours and will accept none. We insist, I repeat *insist*, on paying for our mistakes—*in toto*," he added firmly.

Timothy gurgled in full agreement. The offending ♣ 2, now an exposed card, was duly led and ruffed by R.R. Two tricks were transferred to declarer's side, but there was no longer an entry to dummy's clubs and the Hog was compelled to concede two diamonds, losing six tricks in all, the black aces, two club ruffs and two diamonds. One down. These were the four hands:

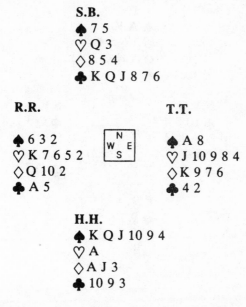

S.B.
♠ 7 5
♡ Q 3
◇ 8 5 4
♣ K Q J 8 7 6

R.R.
♠ 6 3 2
♡ K 7 6 5 2
◇ Q 10 2
♣ A 5

T.T.
♠ A 8
♡ J 10 9 8 4
◇ K 9 7 6
♣ 4 2

H.H.
♠ K Q J 10 9 4
♡ A
◇ A J 3
♣ 10 9 3

"Curious hand," observed Oscar the Owl. "Each defender gives the other a ruff in the same suit."

"The oddest part about it," remarked Peregrine the Penguin, "is that the law, as it stands, is on the side of the culprit. There is no remedy and no redress for the victim. Not at rubber bridge. Now at duplicate . . ."

Fourteenth of the Suit

Still muttering dark imprecations under his breath, the Hog cut out at the end of the rubber. A nervous young Griffin, who took his place, drew the Emeritus Professor, while the Toucan once more faced the Rabbit.

T.T. dealt, opened 1 ◇ and promptly raised the Rabbit's 1 NT to 3 NT.

T.T.
♠ A K
♡ 7 6 5 4
◇ A K Q 10 2
♣ A 3

N.Y.G.
♠ 10 8 4 3 2
♡ A K 2
◇ 5 4
♣ 6 5 2

S.B.
♠ Q J
♡ 10 9 8 3
◇ J 9 7 6
♣ Q J 4

R.R.
♠ 9 7 6 5
♡ Q J
◇ 8 3
♣ K 10 9 8 7

West	North	East	South
—	1 ◇	Pass	1 NT
Pass	3 NT		

"I hope I have enough for you," said the Toucan, tabling his hand. The Hideous Hog, who was kibitzing against the Secretary Bird, greeted the remark with a loud guffaw.

The Nervous Young Griffin opened the ♡ K, and noting the Professor's ten, continued with the ace and deuce. The defence proceeded to take the first four tricks, declarer discarding two clubs from his hand and the deuce of diamonds from dummy on the fourth heart. At trick five, S.B. led a spade to the ace. The Rabbit cashed the ♠ K, as well, and started on the diamonds. As he came to the queen he felt another card sticking to the back and suddenly the ♡ 4 appeared on the green baize.

"Now you should have enough for him," jeered the Hog, "but even against the Professor, twelve cards do not quite constitute adequate notrump support. Ha! Ha!"

"Should I play it at the first opportunity?" asked the Rabbit hesitantly, taken aback by his discovery.

"Certainly," said the Hog, nodding vigorously.

S.B. hissed venomously, but on the spur of the moment he could think of no legal objection, and as he searched for a discard he saw himself hopelessly squeezed in the minors. Hoping to find his partner with the ♣ 10, he threw the four and, much to the Rabbit's surprise, the ♣ Q J came down on his ace and king.

"Unusual type of squeeze," observed O.O. "The menace card is the fourteenth of a suit, so to speak."

With a triumphant leer, H.H. waved the book of Laws at the Secretary Bird.

"To refresh your memory, Professor," he said, addressing him in his silkiest voice, "allow me to read to you that pregnant passage on page 34 which says that dummy cannot revoke. Here we are. Section 63, subsection (c). 'There is no penalty if . . .' "

Chapter 3
MONSTERS IN MASTERS'
CLOTHING

A feature of the three cases submitted to the Monster Points Committee at its first meeting was that, as plaintiff or defendant, Papa the Greek, the Hog's traditional enemy, was each time one of the *dramatis personæ*. The Hideous Hog, who, as our technical adviser, prepares the agenda, dismissed this lightly as a mere coincidence. But cynics remain unconvinced, more especially in view of persistent rumours that H.H. has been betting heavily on Papa to win the dubious distinction of becoming the first Life Monster.

In the first of the cases before us, Papa demanded that Monster Points be inflicted, first against Charlie the Chimp, who was declarer, and next against his own partner, the Emeritus Professor of Bio-Sophistry, known, on account of his personal appearance and curious habits, as the Secretary Bird.

This was the evidence:

Dealer South—Love All

H.H.
♠ J 7.2
♡ J 10 5
◇ A Q J 10
♣ J 8 4

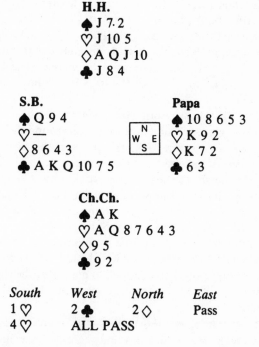

S.B.
♠ Q 9 4
♡ —
◇ 8 6 4 3
♣ A K Q 10 7 5

Papa
♠ 10 8 6 5 3
♡ K 9 2
◇ K 7 2
♣ 6 3

Ch.Ch.
♠ A K
♡ A Q 8 7 6 4 3
◇ 9 5
♣ 9 2

South	West	North	East
1 ♡	2 ♣	2 ◇	Pass
4 ♡	ALL PASS		

The Emeritus Professor, who was West, led out the three top clubs and as the third one hit the table, Papa, East, was ready with a complete analysis of the entire deal. Even allowing for the Chimp's natural optimism, he couldn't have less for his 4 ♡ rebid than the ♠ A K and seven hearts. With three trumps out against him, the finesse would be obligatory, so that the ◇ K would be the third and last trick which the defence could hope to win. It seemed to be a hopeless situation in which any ordinary player would concede defeat gracefully, shrug his shoulders and think of the next deal.

Not so Papa. Quickly conjuring up an irresistible force to break the immovable contract, he proceeded to ruff his partner's master club with the ♡ 9, proclaiming to the world that he was bent on trump promotion. Partner, it is true, couldn't have a trump; and a void offers, admittedly, little scope for promotion. But the Chimp wasn't to know that. Theoretically Papa might hope to find the Professor with, say, ♡ Q x, in which case ruffing with the nine would set up a trick. That, at any rate, was what the Chimp was intended to think, and once only two trumps were out against him, there was no reason to finesse. The better play would surely be to lay down the ♡ A in the hope of dropping West's king.

The Chimp duly overruffed the ♡ 9 with the queen and, before continuing, paused to study the vibrations round the table. Papa had a faraway, distrait look. His partner, the Secretary Bird, showed none of the tenseness to be expected of a player who was waiting anxiously to score a vital trick with a singleton king. These were straws in the wind, significant but inconclusive, and before coming to a decision, the Chimp embarked on what might be described as a discovery play. Slowly stretching his hand out towards dummy, he let his fingers hover gently over the ♡ J.

"If it's not too much trouble," hissed the Secretary Bird, "perhaps you will be good enough to play from the right hand."

"Thank you Professor, thank you very much," said the Chimp gratefully.

That was all he wanted to know, for surely the Professor, obsessed as he was with rules and regulations, wouldn't try to stop him taking the finesse if he had the singleton king of trumps poised over the ace. The Chimp glanced at Papa for confirmation. No longer distrait, the Greek was generating hatred with every breath. A pedant, preoccupied with procedural niceties, had brutally torn to shreds a beautiful piece of deception. A work of art had been desecrated.

The Chimp lost a trick to the ◊ K, but finessed successfully against the king of trumps and triumphantly brought home his contract.

It was against this lurid background that Papa brought forward twin charges: sharp practice against the Chimp, vandalism against the Secretary Bird.

The Hideous Hog, who had been Charlie's partner, asked leave of the Committee to defend the Chimp.

"Since I was dummy," began H.H., "my complete impartiality is not in doubt and I can speak freely. What actually happened, gentlemen? In a critical situation, my good friend Themistocles put his faith in subtlety and finesse. These are his natural weapons. His opponent, the Chimp, less gifted, no doubt, resorted to, er, a little low cunning. That is *his* natural weapon. Honours, therefore, are roughly even, so should we not take a charitable view, bearing in mind that justice was done in the end? Oh yes, that quibbler and incurable meddler, the Emeritus Professor, has been rightly punished. True, my friend has suffered in the process, but we should have the courage and self-discipline to bear his misfortunes stoically."

Though the Committee's decision is still awaited, Charlie the Chimp enjoys already, in all but name, the exalted status of a Master Monster.

H.H. Pleads for Justice

Who wins when the worst contract runs up against the worst defence? This strange confrontation gave birth to the second case brought before our Committee. The scene was the regular Thursday-night duplicate at the Unicorn.

Opposing Papa and Karapet, the Free Armenian, who sat East-West, were two newcomers. Sitting North, with a glazed look and a goatee beard, was the distinguished author of twenty-eight unpublished books. Facing him was a keyhole manufacturer, reputed to be the biggest in the business.

This was the fateful board:

Dealer South—N/S Vulnerable

D.A.
♠ 10 9 8 2
♡ K J 7 6
◇ K J 6 3
♣ Q

Papa
♠ K 7 6 4
♡ 10 9 5
◇ 9 8
♣ A J 9 7

```
    N
 W     E
    S
```

Karapet
♠ Q J 3
♡ 8 4 3 2
◇ 4
♣ K 5 4 3 2

K.M.
♠ A 5
♡ A Q
◇ A Q 10 7 5 2
♣ 10 8 6

South	West	North	East
1 ◇	Pass	3 ◇	Pass
3 ♠	Pass	4 ♠	Dble
Redble	Pass	Pass!	

The bidding sequence, being somewhat unorthodox, calls perhaps for explanation. This is what transpired at the post-mortem.

South's 3 ♠ was something between a cue bid, a waiting bid, and a slam try. When North, mistaking it for a genuine suit, bid 4 ♠, it looked to Karapet as if opponents were sailing gaily to a slam, and to indicate a helpful lead, he doubled. To the keyhole tycoon, caught in the coils of North's unforeseeable spade raise, the double came as a happy release. He didn't know what to do over 4 ♠, for anything he said, even 5◇, might be mistaken for a cue bid, agreeing spades as trumps. There seemed to be no means of escape—until suddenly Karapet's heavensent double opened the perfect way out. A redouble would tear the scales from partner's eyes and force him to bid. Even the distinguished author would surely see that no sane South could want to stay in 4 ♠ redoubled.

North, alas, wasn't with it. Any doubts he may have had about the spade suit originally were set at rest. Clearly, he said to himself, South wouldn't have redoubled were he not happy to play in 4 ♠.

The play was no less curious than the bidding. Capturing Papa's ♡ 10 with the ace, declarer led a diamond to dummy's king and continued with the ♠ 10. There being no hope of promotion, Karapet played low, while Papa, confident that his ♠ K couldn't run away, allowed the ♠ 10 to hold.

Declarer now led a diamond which Karapet didn't ruff, in case Papa had the ace. Having collected the first four tricks, South cashed the ♠ A and exited with a diamond. Papa ruffed and promptly laid down the ♠ K to draw two trumps for one. The reverse happened, however, for it was Karapet, and not declarer, who produced the missing trump. Now dummy's fourth spade put South in full control, and after conceding a trick to the ♣ A, he could claim the rest.

"Why didn't you ruff that second diamond?" demanded Papa.

"Was that a good reason for butchering my ♠ Q?" countered Karapet.

And yet it wasn't such a good board for North-South. At some tables the lay-down slam in diamonds was bid and made, and the Hideous Hog, who was one of the victims, again asked leave to address the Committee.

"I have a duty to my partner," he explained. "Besides, there's such a thing as fair play. An abominable contract has succeeded against an abominable defence. I do not blame Papa. Only a first-class player—and who would accuse him of being that—would know how to defend after such a bidding sequence. For all that, it would be a gross injustice if North-South's lamentable performance were rewarded with a good score. Not being members of the club, they are, unfortunately, ineligible for Monster Points. The only fair solution in the circumstances would be, I submit, to cancel the board, revise the scores in retrospect, and redistribute the prizes."

The Hog, who would have won the event but for the board in question, has let it be known unofficially that his partner would be prepared, as a compromise, to accept the silver-backed hairbrushes which have been earmarked as the first prize for the following week's duplicate.

A Monster's Master Coup

Yet another episode in the long-standing feud between the Hideous Hog and Papa the Greek provided the dramatic setting for the last of the three cases submitted to the Monster Points Committee. To add colour to the event, the Rueful Rabbit appeared as the Hog's partner, while Karapet, confidently expecting the worst, faced Papa.

This was the hand which the Committee was asked to study:

Dealer North—E/W Vulnerable
N/S 60

H.H.
♠ A 9 5 3
♡ A
◇ A K Q J
♣ A 9 5 3

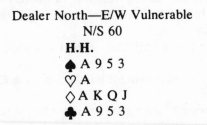

Karapet
♠ 8 7 6 4
♡ 10 9 8 7
◇ 10
♣ 8 7 6 4

Papa
♠ K Q J 10
♡ K Q J
◇ 8 7
♣ K Q J 10

R.R.
♠ 2
♡ 6 5 4 3 2
◇ 9 6 5 4 3 2
♣ 2

North	East	South	West
2 ♣	Pass	2 ◇	Pass
Pass!	3 ◇	4 ◇	Pass
Pass	Dble	Pass	4 ♠
5 ◇	5 ♠	Pass	Pass
6 ◇	6 ♠	Pass	Pass
Dble	Redble	7 ◇	Dble

As the Hog opened 2 ♣, an involuntary shudder shook Papa's frame. Yet apart from a low choking sound at the back of his throat, he showed no sign of emotion. Only when H.H. passed the Rabbit's conventional 2 ◇ did the Greek, nostrils dilated and eyes ablaze, enter the fray. There was a villainous one-man plot against him. Taking advantage of the part-score, the Hog was trying to talk him out of a game, maybe even a slam. No doubt he had a string of diamonds and expected his specious 2 ♣ opening to intimidate Papa—Papa of all people! Well, he would show him. Such was the overture to an auction which soon thundered into the slam zone.

It should be said in fairness to the Hog that not for a single moment did he expect the Rabbit to make 5 ◇, let alone six. But knowing Papa, he could rely on him, once his blood was up, to bid on dauntlessly.

The Greek, for his part, redoubled 6 ♠, not so much because he expected Karapet to win twelve tricks, as to show the world, and more especially the Hog, that he was not to be trifled with.

The cost of the exercise had to be weighed against the prospect that, overawed by the redouble, the Rabbit would panic and run to 7 ◇, which is precisely what happened.

"You called 6 ◇ yourself," he pleaded as with a vicious snarl the Hog tabled the dummy. "And if it's worth sacrificing against a mere game, it's surely worth another 200 to save a slam. I mean, I only bid one more."

Karapet, who had doubled primarily to stop Papa from bidding 7 ♠, opened the ◇ 10. There was nothing the Rabbit liked better than ruffing when there were plenty of trumps about, and he set to with gusto, ruffing everything in sight.

First came the ♠ A and a spade ruff, then the ♡ A and another spade ruff. A heart ruff, the ♣ A, a club ruff and another heart ruff followed in quick succession. At trick ten another club was ruffed in the closed hand, leaving this position:

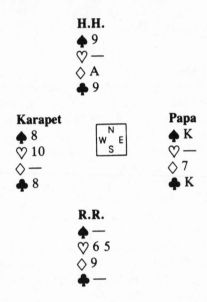

H.H.
♠ 9
♡ —
◇ A
♣ 9

Karapet
♠ 8
♡ 10
◇ —
♣ 8

Papa
♠ K
♡ —
◇ 7
♣ K

R.R.
♠ —
♡ 6 5
◇ 9
♣ —

As the Rabbit led a heart to the eleventh trick, the Greek showed him his hand. "Shall we say one down?" he asked pleasantly. "You can ruff that heart in dummy, and you have a trump left in your hand to take care of one of dummy's losers, but then my trump comes into its own and . . ."

"What!" roared the Hog. "Are you trying to bamboozle my partner, to do him out of a cold grand slam?"

"Which, may I ask, do you claim as your thirteenth trick?" demanded Papa in menacing tones.

"Play to the eleventh and I will tell you the thirteenth," retorted the Hog.

Papa detached the ♣ K, hastily restored it to his hand and tried the ♠ K, only to put it back again quickly. Whichever king he discarded, the nine in that suit would be master and he would have to throw on it his other king, or else ruff and be over-ruffed.

"Why did you double?" he cried indignantly, turning to Karapet.

"Why didn't you let them play it in 2 ◇?" replied the Free Armenian.

All agreed that Papa richly deserved a Monster Point for his performance. But as we left the Committee meeting, Oscar the Owl said thoughtfully to Peregrine the Penguin: "Some great mathematician once worked out, I believe, that if two monkeys banged on a piano for a billion years, sooner or later they would come to play Beethoven's entire Fifth Symphony. Well, that's just what seems to have happened to that Rabbit. He bids out of fright, and shutting his eyes, strikes at random a series of notes, thirteen to be precise, and it all adds up to a grand slam on a rare type of squeeze."

"A Monster in Master's clothing," commented the Penguin.

Chapter 4

THE RABBIT TAKES THE BISCUIT

"They tend to go to his head," said Oscar the Owl.

Peregrine the Penguin nodded gravely in agreement.

"And yet, to be fair to him," resumed O.O., "he only munches them to give himself something to think about while he is playing, something to occupy his mind."

We were talking about the Rueful Rabbit and his habit of nibbling chocolate almond biscuits during the play of the hand. This had become more pronounced of late, and we all felt that it was affecting his game.

Only the day before a vulnerable grand slam came up which, we felt sure, the Rabbit would neither have bid nor made had it not been for those biscuits:

Dealer North—Game All

T.T.
♠ A 10 8 7
♡ A Q 3
◇ K 3
♣ K Q 8 7

W.W.
♠ J 5
♡ 10 9 8 7
◇ 7 6 4
♣ J 10 9 5

Papa
♠ Q 3 2
♡ 6 5 4
◇ Q 10 8 5
♣ 6 3 2

R.R.
♠ K 9 6 4
♡ K J 2
◇ A J 9 2
♣ A 4

South	North
—	1 ♣
2 ♠	3 ♠
4 ♣	4 NT
5 ♠	5 NT
6 ♠	7 ♠

If the bidding sequence seems far from clear, it is largely because the Toucan was asking questions in Blackwood and the Rabbit was replying to them in Gerber.

His long, red nose aglow with excitement, T.T. bounced wildly in his chair when he heard that partner had three aces and three kings. With controls to spare, there was nothing left to investigate and the Toucan went straight to 7 ♠. "A gross underbid," whispered Colin the Corgi, who was kibitzing against Papa.

"You will like my hand," announced T.T. proudly as he tabled his cards, beaming in all directions. First came the hearts, then the spades, next to them the diamonds and finally the clubs, describing a pretty pattern of red suits alternating with black.

The Walrus opened the ♡ 10 and the Rabbit tried to count his tricks. Even allowing for a lucky break in diamonds the total would not exceed eleven, twelve at the most. The situation clearly called for a squeeze and this, in turn, demanded a rectification of the count, but though the Rabbit had bought many books on the technique of squeeze play, including one in Italian and another which he thought was probably in Dutch or Swedish, he couldn't think of any trick that he could lose conveniently without jeopardising his contract.

Winning the heart lead in his hand, he decided ·to test the diamonds immediately. The deuce to the king in dummy was followed by the three to the A J 9. The jack held, so all was well—so far. To trick four the Rabbit led the ◇ A, on which he flicked dummy's ♠ 7. Ignoring the murmurs of surprise round the table and noting Papa's queen, R.R. went on with the ◇ 9, hoping for the best.

It is laid down in all the most authoritative treatises that if a particular distribution is needed to bring home a difficult contract then, regardless of the odds against it, declarer should play for that distribution. The Rabbit now played for the ◇ 9 to be high. He was trying to work out the chances mathematically when the Walrus and two kibitzers, speaking in unison, pointed out that the lead was in dummy. With a club to the ace R.R. returned to the closed hand and again played the ◇ 9, tossing on it the ♠ 8 from the table. East produced the ◇ 10, but once more everyone insisted that the lead was in dummy, and the Rabbit didn't like to argue. He had been wrong too often in things like that before to trust his judgment implicitly. With his ♣ 4 he crossed to the table and cashed the ♣ K and ♣ Q, then the ♡ A and ♡ Q, leaving this position:

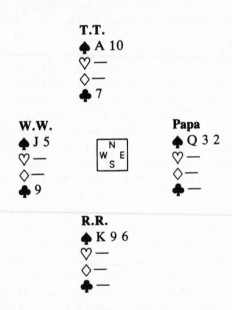

On the ♣ 7 Papa, much to the Rabbit's surprise, went up with the ♠ Q. The play made no sense. "No clubs?" he asked in a weak voice.

"If I had a club, I wouldn't have ruffed, would I?" snapped the Greek irritably.

"Ruff?" repeated the Rabbit, more bemused than ever. "But you can't. I mean, you haven't a trump. I am in 7 NT, so . . ."

"The contract happens to be 7 ♠," broke in the exasperated Greek.

"No, no," protested R.R. "Notrumps is the agreed suit. I only bid spades *en passant* to show my aces and kings, and besides, hearts, not spades, were on dummy's right, but of course no one bid hearts. Surely," went on the Rabbit, "you don't think I would have ruffed my own tricks had the contract been 7 ♠, do you?"

The Rabbit defended himself stubbornly, for he did not like to appear ridiculous. But every hand was raised against him. His own partner, the Toucan, maintained that the bid was 7 ♠, and eventually he was forced to give away.

Covering the queen of trumps with the king, he led the ♠ 6. West followed with the ♠ 5 and R.R. finessed. He could hardly help himself, for Papa had two cards left, both being spades, and if he had the jack, it couldn't drop.

"The Devil's Coup by the Guardian Angel," observed Colin the Corgi.

"Made heavy weather of it, I must say," spluttered the indignant Walrus. "With my two points, I expected you to put your hand down at trick one."

Furtively the Rabbit looked for a biscuit, but the plate was empty. With a vicious look, Papa was swallowing the last one.

R.R. Plays *à la* Hog

Again it is on record that the Rabbit munched through an entire plate of biscuits in bringing off a previously unknown coup during a recent rubber with the Hog against Papa and the Walrus.

This was the hand:

Dealer North—Love All

H.H.
♠ A 7 4 3 2
♡ 4 3 2
♢ A 3 2
♣ A 2

W.W.
♠ 5
♡ Q J 10
♢ 8 7 6 5
♣ 8 7 6 5 3

Papa
♠ Q J 10 9 8
♡ —
♢ K J 10 9
♣ K J 10 9

N
W E
S

R.R.
♠ K 6
♡ A K 9 8 7 6 5
♢ Q 4
♣ Q 4

North	South
1 ♠	3 ♡
3 NT	5 ♡
6 ♡	

I was rather perplexed at the time by Rabbit's bid of 5 ♡, and I asked him afterwards what it meant.

"I wanted to check on aces," he explained.

"Shouldn't you, then, have called 4 NT?"

"Oh no," said the Rabbit firmly. "The Hog would have passed. You see, he had called notrumps first. He always does, of course, and that means that he need only pass a Blackwood 4 NT to make sure of playing the hand."

Walter the Walrus, who was West, opened the queen of trumps on which Papa dropped the nine of diamonds. After a long and painful huddle, the Rabbit ducked. Another heart followed and the Rabbit, who had now formed his plan of campaign, sprang to life. With ten tricks only in sight and two more needed from nowhere, the situation, as he explained later, called for the Hog technique, and there and then, R.R. decided to play the hand *à la* Hog.

Whenever H.H. reeled off a long suit, and he seemed to hold longer and more reelable suits than other people, someone invariably threw a trick at him. That was a squeeze. When the same thing happened again, it was a progressive squeeze. That's what was required now, and the Rabbit set out to do it.

Winning the second trick with the ace, he thrust heart after heart at the enemy's solar plexus. What was more, he noticed some of the discards. From dummy he shed the deuce of clubs and the two baby diamonds. Papa let go the ten of diamonds, the nine and the ten of clubs and the nine of spades. On the sixth round of hearts the Greek parted with the jack of diamonds. R.R.'s delicate nostrils quivered with excitement. Could it be that Papa had been forced to bare the king of diamonds? Unable to contain his curiosity, he led a low diamond to dummy's ace and as the king came tumbling down, his heartbeats quickened. With a spade, on which Papa played the ten, he crossed back to his hand to lead the queen of diamonds. The Greek discarded the jack of spades, leaving this four-card position.

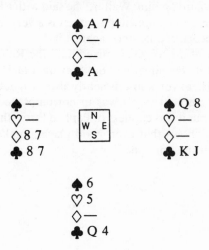

The Rabbit, who had seen the ten and nine of spades precede the jack, was about to claim the rest. Caution, however, prevailed, and to make quite sure that the spades were good he led the six to dummy's ace. When Papa dropped the queen he beamed with pleasure for had he not brought home *à la* Hog an impossible contract?

His triumph was shortlived. The eight of spades, cunningly concealed by the Greek, now came into its own to beat dummy's seven. Taken aback, the Rabbit threw the five of hearts on the table with a gesture of irritation. Shrugging his shoulders petulantly, he said: "One down. Of course I should have played my last heart first before touching spades. Then Papa would have been truly squeezed and I would have made my 6 NT. Sorry."

"I forgive you," said the Hog magnanimously, "for at this point there is nothing even you can do to lose the contract, which is, incidentally, 6 ♡. I know you do not bother about such trivia, but I congratulate you just the same, for you played well, if without malice aforethought."

"Why did you discard that jack of diamonds?" asked the Walrus, looking reproachfully at Papa.

Before the Greek could reply, Oscar intervened: "You mustn't be too hard on him, Walter," he said with a kindly smile. "A trump squeeze in a notrump contract is a very unusual play. There is no recognised defence against it."

"It was silly of me to get so mixed up," the Rabbit admitted ruefully when it was all over, "but playing *à la* Hog is a little confusing. H.H., as you know, is nearly always in notrumps and I thought for a moment that I was in notrumps, too. Luckily it didn't matter, but it was careless of Papa to throw that diamond, wasn't it? Just shows that even good players make these mistakes. I am not the only one."

Chapter 5

H.H. IN THE MONSTER POINTS RACE

The race to become the first Life Monster is gathering momentum. Leading the field until last week was the Emeritus Professor of Bio-Sophistry, better known as the Secretary Bird. Now Charlie the Chimp has come up with a rush, and it has become a very open race. The Chimp talks bridge well, though far too often, and can concentrate at will on any hand except the hand he happens to be playing.

A Four-Suit Squeeze

This was the gist of the case submitted against him to the Monster Points Committee.

Charlie the Chimp, shown as East in the diagram below, was playing with the Secretary Bird against the Rueful Rabbit, South, and Timothy the Toucan. First the Professor went down in 2 ♡, then the Rabbit went down in 3 ♠. The Chimp, always a restless dummy, was kibitzing a 4 ♠ contract at the next table.

"Unbeatable," he explained while the Rabbit was dealing the third hand of the rubber. "Even with a diamond lead you must come to ten tricks on a dummy reversal because . . ."

"One notrump," announced the Rabbit, breaking in:

T.T.
♠ A 10 8 7
♡ A K 8 7
◇ K Q J 9
♣ 7

Ch.Ch.
♠ J 9 3 2
♡ Q J 3 2
◇ 7 6 2
♣ K Q

S.B.

```
  N
W   E
  S
```

R.R.

South	West	North	East
1 NT	Pass	2 ♣	Pass
2 ◇	Pass	6 NT	

"What sort of notrump are you playing?" asked the Chimp.

"Weak," said the Rabbit.

"Strong," said the Toucan.

"But, surely Timothy," protested R.R., "we always play Acol, a 12–14 notrump nonvulnerable and 16–18 vulnerable."

"But we *are* vulnerable," rejoined T.T.: "why, you've just made 4 ♠ on a dummy reversal and . . ."

"No, no, that was at the next table," said the Rabbit reproachfully; "you're not concentrating, Timothy."

The Secretary Bird led the ♣ 10 and the Toucan, tabling his hand, subsided with a guilty look.

The Rabbit won the first trick with ♣ A and started briskly on the diamonds, the ◇ K, the ◇ Q and the ◇ J, which he overtook with the ◇ A in the closed hand. His mind focused, no doubt, on some other hand, the Chimp threw the ♡ 2 on the third round of diamonds. The Secretary Bird, after following twice, shed two low clubs.

The Rueful Rabbit screwed his eyes the better to concentrate. He knew that good players could count people's hands, and he was trying hard to get a count on dummy. Something, somewhere, didn't quite add up.

Meanwhile, the Chimp was in trouble. Too late, he realised that he had revoked. The problem was how best to recover. If he followed suit with that little diamond, a couple of seconds after showing out, he would be shouting 'Guilty', from the rooftops. And if he held on to the diamond, what could he throw in its place?

The lead marked declarer with the ♣ J, so there could be no question of letting go the ♣ K. The Rabbit had revealed 9 points in the minors—the two aces and the ♣ J, by inference—so he needed 3–5 more to make up the values for his 1 NT. Since he had nothing in hearts, he had to have the ♠ K, and maybe the ♠ Q too. What, then, should the Chimp throw on the fourth round of diamonds, a heart or a spade?

The Chimp reasoned that since declarer's 2 ◇ response to Stayman denied a four-card major, there was a reasonable chance that the Emeritus Professor might have three hearts headed by the ten or nine. That would be enough to stop the suit. In what was admittedly a close decision, one consideration tilted the balance. There was no point in seeking the limelight, and a red card falling on a diamond would be less conspicuous than a black one. So, gripped in the deadly vice of a four-suit squeeze, Charlie the Chimp let go a second heart.

Having finished with the diamonds, the Rabbit led the ♡ 10, then the ♡ 9, and as the ♡ J and ♡ Q fell on the ace and king, his ears tingled with pleasurable excitement. He could see his way to eleven tricks, more than he usually collected in a slam.

On the third heart the luckless Chimp discarded a spade. If the Secretary Bird had the ♠ Q, all might still be well. But from the fourth heart there could be no escape. Hopelessly squeezed in the black suits, Charlie the Chimp had to concede defeat, and the Rueful Rabbit ended by making all thirteen tricks. This was the deal in full:

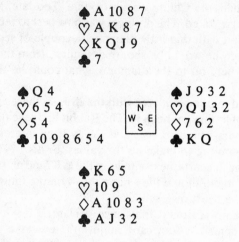

♠ A 10 8 7
♡ A K 8 7
◇ K Q J 9
♣ 7

♠ Q 4
♡ 6 5 4
◇ 5 4
♣ 10 9 8 6 5 4

♠ J 9 3 2
♡ Q J 3 2
◇ 7 6 2
♣ K Q

♠ K 6 5
♡ 10 9
◇ A 10 8 3
♣ A J 3 2

"Do you know," observed the Rabbit ruefully after scrutinising the Chimp's last three cards, "I felt all along that there must be a little diamond about somewhere."

The wild tufts of hair over the Secretary Bird's ears bristled with anger. "No doubt," he hissed "someone at the next table was out of diamonds. How often did they revoke?"

With pen and paper, talking to himself busily, the Rabbit was engrossed in complex calculations. "Thirteen tricks comes to 220 and two revokes at 30 a time adds up to, say, 120, bringing up the grand total to 330, or is it 340. Let's check. Seventeen tricks at . . . ."

"Curious hand," remarked Oscar the Owl, our Senior Kibitzer. "Declarer has only nine tricks, so that even allowing two more tricks for the revoke, he goes one down. But the second revoke creates a progressive pseudo-squeeze which, in the event, is worth four tricks to declarer. Very unusual," concluded O.O., "to find a defender produce the menace card against himself."

The Ethics Committee, which had referred the case to us, reprimanded the Chimp for trying to conceal one revoke by another, an unworthy maneouvre which couldn't go unpunished.

The Chimp, appearing in his own defence, argued that an

extended revoke, such as his, did not amount to a second one. Alternatively, he pleaded the right to withdraw both revokes.

Meanwhile, the Chimp's performance has qualified for the maximum number of Monster Points. Whether he has earned them honestly or not is debatable, but all the Griffins agree that he richly deserves them.

A Vandal at Large

The next case to come before the Monster Points Committee was a straightforward accusation of vandalism by Papa the Greek against Timothy the Toucan. The charge somewhat surprised us, for Timothy, meek, mild and inoffensive, has never aspired to mediocrity and has none of the qualities which go to the making of a monster.

"That Toucan," declared the Greek, "brutally defaced what was, in the bridge sense, a work of art."

This was the deal on which the deed was perpetrated.

Dealer South

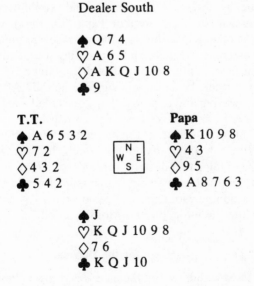

♠ Q 7 4
♡ A 6 5
◇ A K Q J 10 8
♣ 9

T.T.
♠ A 6 5 3 2
♡ 7 2
◇ 4 3 2
♣ 5 4 2

Papa
♠ K 10 9 8
♡ 4 3
◇ 9 5
♣ A 8 7 6 3

♠ J
♡ K Q J 10 9 8
◇ 7 6
♣ K Q J 10

South	North
1 ♥	3 ◊
3 ♥	4 ♥
4 NT	6 ♥

The Toucan, sitting West, opened the ♠ A. What could Papa do to defeat the contract? The question was purely theoretical, and before we could consider the answer, Papa gave it.

"First I asked myself," he explained, "whether declarer could have two losing spades and I decided that it was unlikely, if not impossible. But of one thing I could be certain. He must have a losing club, for with a void he would not have applied Blackwood. The slam, don't forget, had not been bid rationally. It was a wild shot on North's part, so there was no reason why it should succeed against good defence.

"But how could I induce the Toucan to switch to a club? For obviously, unless he did it immediately, it would be too late. If I followed to the ♠ A with the ♠ 8, wouldn't he lead another spade? Would he stop to think that a high card, like the eight, could be my lowest? And even if he did, would he switch? So I made an inspired play," went on Papa. "On the ♠ A I threw the ♠ K! With the ♠ Q in dummy, the message was unmistakable. I was demanding a switch, and demanding it urgently.

"And now, gentlemen," pursued the Greek, "I turn to my alleged partner. What do you suppose he did? After bouncing giddily, swaying and flapping, that Toucan led—a diamond! To him the ♠ K, an unnecessarily high card as he described it, was Lavinthal, a suit-preference signal, calling for the higher-ranking suit. With only three diamonds himself, he must have known from the bidding that declarer couldn't have four. He must have known, too, that with a void in diamonds I would have made a Lightner double. No, there can be no excuse," concluded Papa. "I demand the infliction of a Monster Point."

Case for the Defence

When Papa withdrew and the case was thrown open for discussion, the Hideous Hog unexpectedly entered the fray on behalf of the Toucan.

"Themistocles," he began, "has presented the picture out of focus, a habit of his, I regret to say. The interest of the hand lies not in the flashy play of the ♠ K—sheer exhibitionism, if you ask me—but in North's well-judged jump to 6 ♡. Superficially, it is true, the odds appear to be against bidding a slam with two top losers. But things are not always what they seem, more especially when there is a long, solid suit about to provide the necessary winners.

"There are three possibilities," explained H.H. "If the aces are divided, as was the case, defenders may not discover the true position until it is too late. If West has both aces he will, no doubt, bear in mind that according to some of the best authorities neither should be led. Finally, should East have both aces, West cannot tell which suit to lead. As likely as not, he will open a trump. So, you see, North was only reaping the just reward of his imaginative bidding. His calculated risk had come off, as it deserved to do, and that is all there was to it.

"As you know," continued the Hideous Hog, "I have never professed an exaggerated respect for the Toucan—and any respect at all couldn't fail to be exaggerated—but Papa has only himself to blame. Had he played a low spade there would have been one chance in four, since there are no more than four suits, that the Toucan would have led the right one. These are good odds. To ask for better, playing with him, is sheer greed. No doubt, in calling the slam North had taken into account East's weakness for flamboyant plays. No doubt . . ."

"Who, may I ask, was sitting North?" asked the Owl suspiciously.

"That is quite irrelevant!" retorted the Hog warmly. "Personalities should never be allowed to prejudice the issue."

The case against Timothy the Toucan has been adjourned, but there is a movement afoot to make the Hideous Hog the first Honorary Life Monster.

Chapter 6

KARAPET THE UNLUCKY

"Did I tell you what happened to me on . . ." began Karapet Djoulikyan, the Free Armenian.

"Yes," answered the Corgi and the Walrus in unison, looking hastily at their watches.

Tall, narrow, with a sallow complexion and thick, black eyebrows which met in a permanent frown, Karapet looked like a man who expected the worst in life and who was rarely disappointed. It was common knowledge that the Free Armenian was the unluckiest player on either side of the Equator, and elsewhere, too, no doubt. Not only did he hold atrocious cards, but everything happened to him. Partners fixed him. Opponents excelled against him. The Rabbit had gone an entire afternoon without revoking against him once. Another time, the Walrus did not make a single error, on his own admission, for more than an hour.

Through constant practice Karapet had become a superb loser, but he resented unmannerly people who interrupted him in the recital of his woes, or worse still, preferred to tell their own. More than once he had threatened to emigrate.

"The English are so self-centred," he said to me bitterly after the Corgi and the Walrus had left. "They only want to talk about their own bad luck. Why, they don't know what it is. I could tell them! Now take that 5 ◊ hand I had on Tuesday. It must have been 100–1 against . . ."

I had an urgent phone call to make and could not hear the end of the story. Then someone called "Table Up" and Karapet cut in.

There was a goodly attendance at the Griffins that night. The Grand Slam Sweep, a new feature, was an undoubted success. To encourage the evening game the club had organised a pool to be won by the first pair to call and make a grand slam between 10 and 10.30. A small charge, known as the 'sweep', was imposed daily on every member and the total, doubled by the club, formed the pool.

"There's more than £300 in that sweep," I heard someone say as the players took their seats. The time was 9.55. Karapet faced Papa the Greek, while the Hideous Hog drew the Rueful Rabbit.

I pulled up a chair to kibitz the Hog, who was giving last-minute instructions to the Rabbit: ". . . and let me play the hand sometimes, or rather don't do it yourself. And don't save the rubber, at least not this one. And don't . . ."

Papa was trying to boost Karapet's morale. "Cheer up," he was saying, "things can't be as black as you look." Each side made game. Then this hand came up:

Dealer South—Game All

R.R.
- ♠ A K 9
- ♡ K 7 6
- ◇ A 3 2
- ♣ A J 5 4

Papa
- ♠ J 8 4 2
- ♡ 10 5 4
- ◇ 7 6
- ♣ K 9 3 2

```
   N
 W   E
   S
```

Karapet
- ♠ Q 10 3
- ♡ 3 2
- ◇ J 10 9 8
- ♣ Q 10 7 6

H.H.
- ♠ 7 6 5
- ♡ A Q J 9 8
- ◇ K Q 5 4
- ♣ 8

South	North
1 ♡	3 ♣
3 ◇	3 ♡
4 ♡	4 ♠
5 ♡	6 ♣
6 ◇	7 ♡

Papa picked the ♣ 9 as the most deceptive lead available, and with a guilty look the Rabbit tabled his hand.

"I didn't think we could keep out of six," he tittered, "and with all that money in the pool, over £300, well, I mean, it's worth chancing seven. It's only one more and it's gone ten and . . ."

Hearing the Hog mutter something about "one born every minute and they all cut me", the Rabbit left his sentence unfinished.

The Hideous Hog wasn't listening anyway. He was counting his tricks. He could see eleven, which meant that a player of his calibre could reckon on twelve. But even if the diamonds broke 3–3, against the odds, there was no sign of a thirteenth.

"After all," resumed the Rabbit, looking on the brighter side, "maybe we can't make even six. Then bidding seven can't cost more than 100. I mean, it isn't as if we'd be missing the small slam bonus, for there wouldn't be one, would there?"

"And if you are in real luck," chipped in Colin the Corgi, the facetious young man from Oxbridge, "you can't even get game. That would make the grand slam better than ever, for you could go down happily without missing anything more than a part-score."

While this chatter was in progress, H.H. had formed his plan of campaign. Winning the first trick with the ♣ A, he ruffed a club, crossed to dummy with the ♢ A and ruffed a second club. Then he went back to the table with the ♠ A and ruffed dummy's last club in the closed hand. After playing off the ♡ A Q he went over to dummy once more with a spade to the king. Papa, who had followed to the first spade with the deuce, went up smartly with the jack.

An ordinary player wouldn't have thought of it, but during the post-mortem the Greek pointed out that to an expert such subtle plays came naturally.

"Declarer," he explained, "is counting the hand. The defence should, therefore, try to mislead him. Observe that if he has the ♠ Q, my jack's worthless anyway. But by making him think that I have a doubleton spade, or three at most, I give him a false count

on the diamonds. Partner may have a finessible honour, and it is
my duty to protect him."

After Papa's cunning play of the ♠ J, this was the four-card end
position:

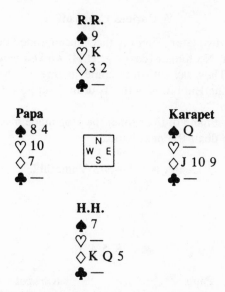

R.R.
♠ 9
♡ K
◇ 3 2
♣ —

Papa
♠ 8 4
♡ 10
◇ 7
♣ —

Karapet
♠ Q
♡ —
◇ J 10 9
♣ —

H.H.
♠ 7
♡ —
◇ K Q 5
♣ —

Completing the dummy reversal, the Hog drew Papa's last
trump with dummy's ♡ K, throwing on it the ♠ 7 from the closed
hand. The luckless Karapet was meanwhile inexorably squeezed
in spades and diamonds.

"Why did you do it to me, Papa?" he cried in injured tones.
"Why did you throw that jack of spades, forcing me to cling to the
queen? First they bid an unmakable grand slam because it's ten
o'clock. Then you make it for them because you're too clever.
Why couldn't you stay stupid for another five minutes? Why do
they always do it to me?"

It was at this point that Papa explained how and why he had to
protect his partner.

The rubber was over and the Rabbit cut out. Thrilled to be the
first winner of the Grand Slam Sweep, he couldn't wait to report
his success to the Club Secretary.

"You've got four without me," he said, picking up his scorecard, duly signed by Papa and Karapet. "I've just seen Timothy show his face round the corner."

A Curious Crossruff

A minute or two later, Timothy the Toucan joined the table and cut the Hog. No longer scowling, H.H. winked genially at the kibitzers. "They say disasters come in threes," he chuckled. "First I cut the Rabbit, now the Toucan. I suppose I'll get Papa next. Ha! ha!"

On the first hand of the rubber the Hog made his usual 3 NT. The Toucan dealt the next hand:

Dealer North—N/S Vulnerable

T.T.
♠ A
♡ Q J 9 8 7
◇ A K
♣ A K 5 4 3

Papa
♠ —
♡ A K 10 6 5 4 3 2
◇ 10 9 8 7
♣ J

Karapet
♠ J 6 5 2
♡ —
◇ Q J 6 3
♣ Q 10 9 8 7

H.H.
♠ K Q 10 9 8 7 4 3
♡ —
◇ 5 4 2
♣ 6 2

South	West	North	East
—	—	1 ♣	Pass
4 ♠	5 ♡	Dble	Pass
5 ♠	Pass	7 ♠	

The bidding requires little comment. The Hog's hand was of a type which offered little scope for individual achievement in defence, and H.H. did not like to play second fiddle to anyone. Hence the 5 ♠ bid. The Toucan felt, for his part, that having missed the biggest penalty of the century, nothing short of a slam could make up for it. He was about to bid six, glanced at the clock—just in time—and hastily made it seven.

"Sorry if I've overstepped the mark a bit," he said with an embarrassed gurgle, putting down his hand, "but there's still a quarter of an hour to go, so I thought we'd have a shot at that sweep. I hear there's nearly £400 in the pool and . . ."

"You're too late," cried Papa and two junior kibitzers. All speaking at once, they informed him that the Grand Slam Sweep had been won a few minutes earlier.

"How was I to know?" complained the Toucan. "No one tells me anything. Of course I would have stopped in six." He was still bouncing in his chair, murmuring apologies, when Papa opened the ♡ K. Karapet discarded the ◇ 3 and the Hog, in a loud aside, deplored the epidemic of insanity which was affecting partners in general and Toucans in particular.

H.H. thought that he could see twelve tricks. Not knowing about the bad trump break, he counted eight spades and dummy's two ace-kings. Could he set up a club for the thirteenth trick? It didn't look like it. Since Karapet had no hearts, he probably held five cards in both minors. There was only one way in which the addition would come to thirteen, and snarling impartially at all around him, H.H. went to work.

After ruffing the ♡ K, he crossed to dummy with a diamond and ruffed another heart. Karapet threw a second diamond, but he still had one left with which to follow to the next trick as H.H. went over again to dummy to ruff a third heart in his hand. The top clubs provided two more entries to ruff dummy's last two hearts. Nine tricks had gone: two diamonds, two clubs and five hearts, and this was the four-card end position:

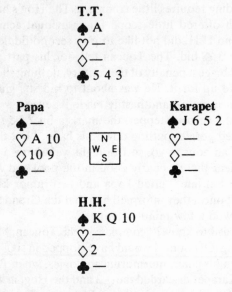

T.T.
♠ A
♡ —
♢ —
♣ 5 4 3

Papa
♠ —
♡ A 10
♢ 10 9
♣ —

Karapet
♠ J 6 5 2
♡ —
♢ —
♣ —

H.H.
♠ K Q 10
♡ —
♢ 2
♣ —

The Hog ruffed his deuce of diamonds with dummy's lone ace of trumps, nodded approvingly as Karapet underruffed, and continued with a club from the table. With nothing left but trumps, the Free Armenian ruffed again.

"Curious hand," observed Oscar the Owl. "In 6 ♠ declarer would almost certainly lose a trump and a diamond and go one down. Yet 7 ♠, as we have just seen, is a make."

"Unusual type of crossruff with a singleton trump in dummy," remarked Peregrine the Penguin.

"Against me," sighed Karapet, "they don't need a trump at all. They can crossruff with a void."

The Crowning Insult

It was Papa's turn to go out. The Rabbit rejoined the table and Karapet cut the Hog.

"Do you know . . ." began the Armenian.

"Yes I do," said the Hog firmly. "I know all about the apocalyptic bad luck which has haunted the Djoulikyans since the

Witch of Ararat put that curse upon them in 1436—or was it '37? Brood on it, if you must, but brood as dummy. Leave the play to me."

On the first hand of the rubber Karapet picked up a 27 count and almost smiled. Then the Rabbit, who had dealt, discovered among his cards the two jokers which he had forgotten to remove from the new pack.

The hand which came up on the redeal was shown round by Karapet at the bar later as an example of the slings and arrows of outrageous fortune to which he was so well accustomed:

Dealer East—Love All

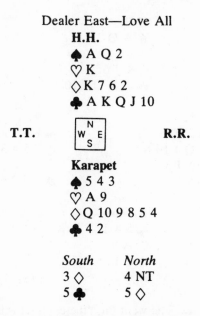

H.H.
♠ A Q 2
♡ K
◇ K 7 6 2
♣ A K Q J 10

T.T.

R.R.

Karapet
♠ 5 4 3
♡ A 9
◇ Q 10 9 8 5 4
♣ 4 2

South	North
3 ◇	4 NT
5 ♣	5 ◇

"I do not blame H.H.," said Karapet magnanimously. "Forgetting with whom he was playing, he hoped to find me with the ace of diamonds, in which case he could see twelve tricks. Hence Blackwood. But, of course, knowing that something, or rather everything, would go wrong I didn't show my ace.

"And now," went on the Armenian, "how do you play the hand in 5 ◇? The lead is the ♡ Q. What do you do at trick two?"

The question was rhetorical, and before anyone could say anything, Karapet resumed with a hollow laugh.

"Don't worry. Whatever you do will be wrong. You lead a trump, but East shows out and your king falls to West's ace. Back comes a spade. If you finesse, the king wins and the spade return locks you in dummy. Should you go up with the ace and lead clubs in the hope of discarding your two losing spades, West will ruff on third round. There's no escape."

Downing his Fernet Branca, the Armenian filled in the other hands:

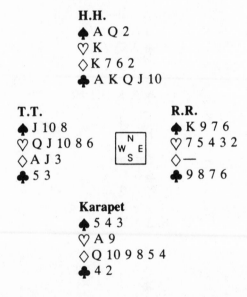

H.H.
♠ A Q 2
♡ K
♢ K 7 6 2
♣ A K Q J 10

T.T.
♠ J 10 8
♡ Q J 10 8 6
♢ A J 3
♣ 5 3

R.R.
♠ K 9 7 6
♡ 7 5 4 3 2
♢ —
♣ 9 8 7 6

Karapet
♠ 5 4 3
♡ A 9
♢ Q 10 9 8 5 4
♣ 4 2

"As you can see," he went on, "the contract is unbreakable, unless the trumps are 3–0 and then only if East has the void and also the ♠ K. And even then you are still home so long as West has three clubs. The odds against everything being wrong must be at least 30–1, and . . ."

"Don't you believe it," broke in the Hog, who had come up to join us. "The odds, though certainly in your favour, were nothing like what you suppose. Your bad luck, my friend, and I am the first to admit it, was that you, not I, happened to be declarer. I usually succeed in protecting my partners against this hazard. This time, alas . . ."

"Are you suggesting," broke in Karapet indignantly, "that you would have made eleven tricks?"

The Hog shook his head. "No, not eleven tricks, twelve, though the extra trick, mind you, would be purely incidental. After that fortunate lead I would have simply ensured my contract which is, needless to say, unbeatable."

"Play," insisted Karapet, determined not to give up his misfortunes lightly.

"Very well, I'll dot the 'is' and cross the 'ts' for you," replied H.H. "At trick two I lead the ◇ 10 and . . ."

"You happen to be in dummy," protested Karapet.

"On the contrary," retorted H.H., "*you* happen to be in dummy, but I happen to be in my hand, for I overtake the ♡ K at trick one to run that ◇10. Let East win with a bare jack, if he has it. He can do no harm and I shall knock out the ◇ A in my own time, before West can lead a spade. And neither your Witch, nor any other, can do a thing about it.

"Of course," concluded the Hog, "it's a very different story on an opening spade lead. Fancy getting a heart! Some people have a charmed life. You lucky devil, Karapet!"

As H.H. walked away, Karapet stood speechless, shaking all over. Never had anything so brutal been said to him before.

Chapter 7

COUPS BY DUMMY

"Nearly ten per cent of the time," sighed the Hideous Hog, "I am dummy. Nature is for ever prodigal and can afford it, I suppose, like the Niagara Falls and all that, but think of the waste!

"Me, dummy, *le mort*, as the French say," went on H.H. bitterly. "Imagine Leonardo without a brush, Newton without an apple, Pasteur without a germ. What frustration!"

Glass after glass, the Hog philosophised on the proper role of dummy in a just society. A triumphant rubber against Papa, shortly before dinner, inspired the disquisition.

Kibitzers from far afield had streamed into the cardroom as the news spread that the Hog had joined the table of his traditional enemy, Papa the Greek. The Toucan and the Rabbit, who made up the four, cut the seven of diamonds. Then they cut again, this time from the same pack, and fate brought H.H. together with R.R. while Papa faced Timothy the Toucan.

On the first hand T.T. opened 1 ◇ and after competing unsuccessfully in notrumps, Papa gave way gracefully to his partner's 3 ◇. The Toucan made ten tricks.

"Barely twelve tricks on top," observed the Hog charitably. "What's more, it needs a certain degree of luck with the hearts. Declarer must guess correctly that his ♡ 10 is master and that there are no more trumps out. No, not a good slam to be in."

After exchanging unfriendly looks with H.H., Papa dealt the next hand and opened 1 NT.

"We have decided to play a strong notrump," announced the Toucan. "Papa's is 16–18 and mine 19–21. I need a wee bit more," he explained, "in case I end up as declarer."

"Not a serious risk with Papa," remarked the Hog in a loud aside.

Holding ♠ A ♡ 6 3 ◇ A K J 7 6 5 4 ♣ 10 9 3 he passed and the auction proceeded:

South	West	North	East
H.H.	T.T.	R.R.	Papa
—	—	—	1 NT
Pass	2 ♠	Pass	Pass
3 ◇	Pass	3 NT	Dble
Pass	4 ♠	Dble	Pass
4 NT	Pass	Pass	Dble

Papa opened the ♣ K, to which the Toucan followed with the ♣ 6 and declarer with the ♣ 7. After a quick look at dummy's powerful diamonds, the Greek switched to the ♠ K, knocking out the ace. The Rabbit took stock. To be more precise, he looked at the ceiling, shook his head, twitched his left nostril and detached a card from his hand.

"You are on the table," warned Papa, quick as lightning.

"What is the meaning of that remark?" asked the Hog, fixing Papa with a malevolent look. "Why, I wonder, are you usurping dummy's customary prerogative?"

"I didn't want to take advantage . . ." began Papa.

"Very sporting," agreed the Rabbit. The Toucan bounced in support.

"Ha!" bellowed the Hog. "He is trying to rob you of three tricks and you call that sporting!"

"But how do you know?" asked the bewildered Toucan. "You don't know what Papa has, or what R.R. has, or even what I have, for that matter."

"On the contrary," retorted H.H., "after that insidious, that 'sporting' warning, I know what you all have."

"And no doubt," broke in Papa, "you could play all our hands better than we could, even without seeing the cards."

"Naturally." The Hog nodded in assent.

"Well then," suggested Papa, twisting his lips in a sardonic smile, "why not play the hand as dummy, calling for the cards from the closed hand? It's not too late to redouble, and we might even have a bottle of your favourite Krug on the result."

"Very generous of you, Themistocles," replied the Hog, "and I will be glad to oblige with a belated redouble, but you'd better make it a magnum of Krug, for our partners, I am sure, would like to join me, after the hand is over, in toasting a gallant loser."

Dummy Takes Over

The Rabbit and the Toucan agreed. Neither knew what was happening, but both liked Krug. The Hog, his hand still exposed, now directed the play. After one club, East's king, and one spade, the king to dummy's bare ace, eleven cards remained.

♠ —
♡ 6 3
♢ A K J 7 6 5 4
♣ 10 9

After a pause to allow the kibitzers to make their bets, the Hog put his left hand to the lapel of his coat and waved the ♢4 aloft in his right. Clearing his throat, he addressed the gathering.

"Before I play this card, the *key* card," he began, "you would doubtless like me to tell you why Mr Papadopoulos was so sporting just now."

Papa spluttered and gesticulated, but all eyes were on the Hog.

"You will recall," he observed, "that declarer was about to play something from the closed hand. Obviously it was a diamond, for with a handsome seven-card suit around, declarer doesn't normally look elsewhere. But the lead was in dummy and someone—Timothy, perhaps, or I might have done it myself—would have pointed it out before a card was played from the table.

"Now you see what it all means, of course," went on H.H., gesturing this way and that with the ♢ 4. "If R.R. had three diamonds, it wouldn't matter what he did. So he clearly had two and his intention was to finesse, not only because Papa had bid 1 NT, but, above all, to keep communications open with dummy.

"Turn to Papa." The ♢4 now pointed at the Greek. "If he had

two diamonds or three to the queen, he couldn't stop the suit anyway, so there would be nothing to gain by being sporting. But suppose that Papa had four diamonds? Imagine his predicament! Having played inadvertently from the closed hand, R.R. would have to lead a diamond from dummy. No longer able to finesse, he could only keep communications open by leading a low diamond, this little four." The Hog now pointed it at the Toucan.

"What happens? East shows out. Without malice aforethought, R.R. has made an advanced safety play, and now the marked finesse on the second round brings him six tricks in diamonds instead of the three he would have made had he played from the right hand."

With a swish the ◇4 descended on the table. Some moments elapsed before the startled Toucan realised that the play had started. Then he searched his hand carefully for a diamond and finding none, discarded the ♣2.

"Follow suit," commanded H.H. The Rabbit extracted the ◇2 and Papa won with the ◇8. He cashed the ♠Q, on which a heart was shed from dummy, and continued with the ♣Q.

"If my hand were not already exposed," chortled the Hog, "I would now table it. Ha! ha! It's all over my friends. Win with the ♣A, R.R., and . . ."

"But how do you know that I've got it?" protested the Rabbit.

"I know everything," replied the Hog modestly, casting down his ginger eyelashes. "You must have two aces, not so much because you bid 3 NT or even because you doubled 4 ♠, for after all, you've been known to do, er, bizarre things before. But don't tell me that Timothy, with an ace in his hand, would have taken out his partner's double of 3 NT into 4 ♠. No, that would be too much. So kindly win the trick with the ♣A and lead a diamond. I claim the rest of the tricks on a double squeeze."

This was the full deal:

R.R.
♠ 10 4 3 2
♡ A J 8 2
◇ 3 2
♣ A 8 7

T.T.
♠ J 9 8 7 6 5
♡ Q 10 9
◇ —
♣ 6 5 4 2

Papa
♠ K Q
♡ K 7 5 4
◇ Q 10 9 8
♣ K Q J

H.H.
♠ A
♡ 6 3
◇ A K J 7 6 5 4
♣ 10 9 3

"Keep your cards up," went on the Hog contemptuously, "while I dot the 'is' and cross the 'ts'." After a few words *sotto voce* with the barman, H.H. turned once more to the kibitzers.

"When I lead my last diamond, I shall be left with two cards, the ♣ 10 and the ♡ 6. Papa will then have to keep the ♣ J. He must have it, of course, for he wouldn't have led the ♣ K from KQ nothing. So he will have room for one heart only. Timothy, playing in front of R.R., can't let go his master spade, so he, too, will be down to one heart. Now I shall call on R.R. to discard a spade and score the last two tricks with his ace and another heart, whatever it may be."

To the barman, who had picked up the phone, the Hog called out: "Make sure it's the '69, Heron." Then he resumed. "Mind you, I don't know who has the ♡ Q. To bring his count up to 16, Papa must have either the ♡ K or the ♡ Q J, but he could have a maximum 1 NT with the ♡ K Q. If so, he alone is squeezed. Basically, it makes no difference and . . ."

"Simple, elementary, automatic squeeze," scoffed Papa; "and

now, perhaps, we can deal the next hand if, that is, you have quite finished gloating."

"Not absolutely, I am afraid." There was a faint note of apology in the Hog's voice. "You did say, I seem to recall, that I could play *all* the hands better than you could, without seeing the cards. You were perfectly right, of course, and I was about to point out that you should have defeated me, breaking up a simple, elementary, automatic squeeze by leading a heart at trick four. Rather sporting of me to redouble in the circumstances, but then one sporting gesture deserves another, I always say."

Any Honours, Partner?

Another striking demonstration of the Hog's prowess in declarer play from across the table occurred soon afterwards in a rubber which saw him, once more in harness with the Rabbit, opposite the Secretary Bird and Walter the Walrus.

The first hand was Walrus-proof, and after blocking one suit and forgetting to cash a winner in another, he made game in notrumps.

Then came this deal, which I watched from a seat behind the Rabbit:

Dealer West—E/W Game

H.H.
♠ J 9
♡ 6 5
◊ A J 10 9 8
♣ K J 9 7

S.B.   **W.W.**

R.R.
♠ A K 10 8 6
♡ Q 4 3
◊ K Q 5
♣ 6 5

After three passes R.R. opened 1 ♠, and this was the brief, uncontested auction:

South	North
1 ♠	2 ◇
2 ♠	3 ♠
Pass	

The Secretary Bird opened with the king and ace of hearts on which his partner, the Walrus, played the jack then the deuce. After a pause the ♣ 4 followed. Which card should the Rabbit play from the table? While he looked at the ceiling for inspiration, I tried to work out the hand.

Why had S.B. switched to clubs after receiving so much encouragement from his partner in hearts? I could think of one reason only: the fear that the Walrus could not overruff dummy, and would thereby give vital information to declarer. That information could only refer to the ♠ Q, and it followed that the S.B. had been dealt that queen singleton, or more likely doubleton. And in that case he was hardly likely to hold an honour in clubs as well, for with an eleven count and a six-card major he would have surely opened the bidding.

It appeared, therefore, that the Rabbit was destined to lose two clubs and that the contract would hinge on his play of the trump suit. Presumably, he would finesse and go one down.

Someone jogged R.R. out of his daydream—I learned later that he was wondering where he had parked his car—and he settled on dummy's ♣ J.

The Walrus won with the queen and returned a trump. Going up with the ace, on which S.B. played the ♠ 7, the Rabbit continued with the ◇ K.

I saw H.H. look up sharply. Why was the Rabbit not drawing trumps? Next to dealing, it was the best part of his game, and there appeared to be no reason at all for the ◇ K. Ominously, the queen followed the king and by this time there could be little doubt that R.R. was playing the hand in notrumps.

The Hog was about to say something, but caught his breath

and waited patiently until a low diamond had been played from dummy.

"Sorry, partner," he said, transferring the jack of spades, which had been nestling between the red suits, to dummy's right. "I always forget."

The hint, however, was wasted. The Rabbit's thoughts were far away, and he was about to continue, automatically, with the ◇5 when the Hideous Hog spoke again.

"Any honours, partner?" he asked.

"Who? What? Honours? N-no, no honours." The spell was broken.

"Your hand," snarled the Hog as R.R. was about to play dummy's ♠ J. After that there was no longer any play for losing the contract.

These were the four hands:

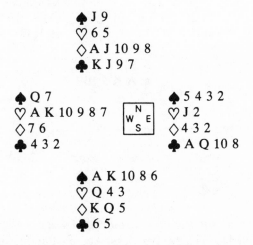

♠ J 9
♡ 6 5
◇ A J 10 9 8
♣ K J 9 7

♠ Q 7   ♠ 5 4 3 2
♡ A K 10 9 8 7   ♡ J 2
◇ 7 6   ◇ 4 3 2
♣ 4 3 2   ♣ A Q 10 8

♠ A K 10 8 6
♡ Q 4 3
◇ K Q 5
♣ 6 5

"You know," the Rabbit told me afterwards in strict confidence, "I had quite forgotten that spades were trumps. But you can see now that the Hog is not as unscrupulous as they make out. He did not breathe a word until it was too late for me to get into dummy to take the trump finesse. Luckily, of course, the queen dropped, but he could not know that, could he?"

Noblesse Oblige

On the next hand the Emeritus Professor went down in 3 NT. Then came this deal:

Dealer East—E/W Vulnerable
N/S 90

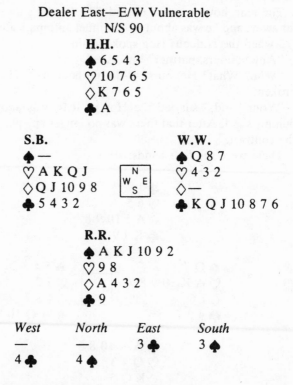

H.H.
♠ 6 5 4 3
♡ 10 7 6 5
◇ K 7 6 5
♣ A

S.B.
♠ —
♡ A K Q J
◇ Q J 10 9 8
♣ 5 4 3 2

W.W.
♠ Q 8 7
♡ 4 3 2
◇ —
♣ K Q J 10 8 7 6

R.R.
♠ A K J 10 9 2
♡ 9 8
◇ A 4 3 2
♣ 9

West	North	East	South
—	—	3 ♣	3 ♠
4 ♣	4 ♠		

Of course S.B. should have bid 5 ♣. Even the Walrus couldn't have failed to make twelve tricks. At unfavourable vulnerability, however, and knowing nothing of the void in diamonds, the Professor feared that a sacrifice wouldn't be worth while, and he wasn't without hope of beating the contract. After all, the Rabbit would be playing the hand.

The king, ace and queen of hearts, in that order, were led to the first three tricks. The Rabbit ruffed on the third round and played his ace of trumps. Seeing West show out, he crossed to dummy's ♣ A to take the marked finesse in trumps.

Back in his hand with the ♠ J, he was about to play the king when the Walrus, setting down a cup of coffee, turned abruptly and jolted R.R's elbow. The ♠ 9, the end card in his hand, dropped accidentally on the table.

"Sorry," apologised the Walrus, "clumsy of me, but they do put these tables in the most awkward . . ."

"My fault, really, I, er . . ." chittered the Rabbit, and he was about to pick up the card when H.H. stopped him.

"I am afraid," he said gently but very firmly, "that the card has been played. Much as it is against our interests, we must observe the rules."

"No, no," protested the Walrus. "It was my fault entirely. I could not possibly take advantage of it. I wouldn't dream . . ."

The S.B. hissed softly. Something was wrong, but what was it?

"Please pick it up," implored W.W.

"Your sentiments do you credit," said the Hog, inclining his head. "*Noblesse oblige*. Nevertheless that card has been played."

The Hog pushed the ♠ 9 towards the Walrus, saying in his silkiest voice: "Play anything, my dear Walter, anything you like. There's no need at all to be embarrassed. It's the luck of the game. Another time it will be in our favour."

Slowly, reluctantly, the Walrus gathered the trick, which had fallen so unexpectedly to his queen of trumps, and having nothing left but clubs, led a club.

The Rabbit discarded a diamond from his hand, trumping the club in dummy, returned to the closed hand with the ◇A, and for want of anything better to do, led out his trumps. On the last one, West was hopelessly squeezed in the red suits, the three-card end position being:

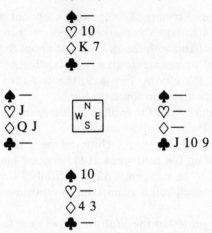

```
              ♠ —
              ♡ 10
              ◇ K 7
              ♣ —
  ♠ —                        ♠ —
  ♡ J          N             ♡ —
  ◇ Q J     W     E          ◇ —
  ♣ —          S             ♣ J 10 9
              ♠ 10
              ♡ —
              ◇ 4 3
              ♣ —
```

The unnatural loss of the trump trick had been compensated at once by the ruff and discard, and at the same time, it rectified the count for a squeeze against S.B. Had the Rabbit ducked a diamond, not that it would have occurred to him, the Secretary Bird could have broken up the squeeze by leading the jack of hearts.

For the squeeze to operate a trick had to be lost, but it had to be lost to East and not to West.

"Excellent dummy play," said the Hog. The Rabbit looked startled. He was not in the habit of receiving compliments. But the Hog was perfectly sincere. He thought that dummy had played very well.

H.H. *v* H.H.

"I often wish," said H.H. as he joined us at the bar later that night, "that I could play against myself. It would be such a good game, you know, though I couldn't afford such high stakes, of course. Why, I'd be ruined."

Oscar the Owl motioned to the barman.

"I'm giving up non-sparkling beverages for Lent . . ." began the Hog.

"But it's not Lent," objected the Toucan, who had a factual approach to life.

"However," went on the Hog, ignoring the interruption, "I'll be glad to join you in a bottle of Krug."

On the back of a Final Demand notice from the Inland Revenue he wrote down a hand.

"There," he said. "You remember my little gam . . . er . . . R.R.'s little gambit in 4 ♠ this afternoon? Well, the very next rubber I cut against Papa and it was another 4 ♠ contract, which made me think how exciting it would be if I could play against myself.

"I'll show you the full deal," he went on, "because as you will soon see for yourselves, declarer and defenders alike could play on double dummy lines. But let's see first whether you would rather be East or West, and just to help you decide, I'll give you the bidding."

The Hog passed round this diagram:

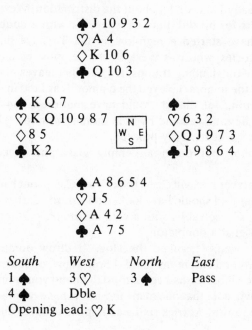

```
              ♠ J 10 9 3 2
              ♡ A 4
              ◇ K 10 6
              ♣ Q 10 3

♠ K Q 7                      ♠ —
♡ K Q 10 9 8 7    N          ♡ 6 3 2
◇ 8 5           W   E        ◇ Q J 9 7 3
♣ K 2             S          ♣ J 9 8 6 4

              ♠ A 8 6 5 4
              ♡ J 5
              ◇ A 4 2
              ♣ A 7 5
```

South	West	North	East
1 ♠	3 ♡	3 ♠	Pass
4 ♠	Dble		

Opening lead: ♡ K

"South appears to have five losers," observed O.O. "Two trumps and one trick in each of the other suits."

"Seems a bit hopeless," ventured the Toucan, bouncing gently on his high stool.

The Hog turned to Colin the Corgi.

"Quite right," agreed C.C., "and therefore I'll back South, for as there would be nothing clever in breaking the contract, I assume that you were South, H.H., and made it, and as you know, I like to be on the winning side. Gloat and the world gloats with you. Moan and you moan alone."

"Since there would be nothing clever in breaking the contract," retorted H.H., "perhaps you would be good enough to do it. I'll be South, as I was this afternoon. I hope that you agree with the lead."

The Corgi nodded.

"I win, noting East's deuce, and I lead a diamond to my ace, then another towards the table," announced the Hog. "Observe that already I know a lot about the distribution. West must have six hearts for his bid, but not seven, for with a doubleton East would have started a high-low signal. To have doubled me, Themistocles, who was West, of course, must be credited with the three outstanding trumps, K Q 7. That leaves him with four cards in the minors. I played the diamonds as I did in case he had a singleton, not that it would have mattered, mind you, but anyway he followed and I was in dummy with the ◇K. At trick four I led a heart. Pray proceed."

The Hog put down an empty glass and picked up his own.

"Whatever I do will cost a trick," said C.C., "but had I not seen all the hands, I should have looked on a third heart as the least of all evils. Conceivably, with a void in trumps, partner might not like to signal a doubleton."

"Very well," resumed the Hog. "I throw dummy's ten of diamonds and ruff in my hand. I now know, of course, that you have two clubs, for had you a third diamond you would have led it. You will note that one of my five losers has evaporated. Watch another vanish. At trick six I lead a spade towards dummy. East shows out, confirming my diagnosis. You are in with one of your trump honours."

"Second throw-in, " observed P.P.

"I return a low club," murmured C.C. weakly.

"I go up with dummy's ♣ Q, cash the ♣ A and we come to this five-card end position," said the Hog:

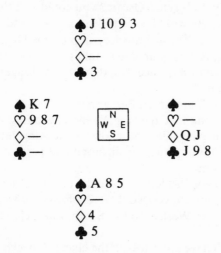

    ♠ J 10 9 3
    ♡ —
    ◇ —
    ♣ 3

♠ K 7   ♠ —
♡ 9 8 7   N   ♡ —
◇ —   W E   ◇ Q J
♣ —   S   ♣ J 9 8

    ♠ A 8 5
    ♡ —
    ◇ 4
    ♣ 5

"I lead my ♠ A and another trump to your king and . . ."

"Third throw-in," remarked O.O. P.P. concurred, nodding gravely.

"Precisely," agreed the Hog. "You have to lead a heart. I throw dummy's club, ruff with my last trump and it's all over. Let me tell you," added H.H., smiling indulgently, "that Papa did better than that. At least he gave himself a chance, which is more than you did."

We held on to our glasses, saying nothing.

"I can see that you are all impatient to know how Papa defended," continued the Hog. "Very well, I'll tell you. He could see well enough what was coming, so when I threw him in with a heart at trick three, he boldly led the ♠ K. Though it cost a trick, it gained two, for he was no longer obliged to give me a ruff and discard and, what's more, he now had an exit card, for the next throw-in. When I returned a trump to his queen, after taking my ace, he could lead the ♠ 7 in perfect safety."

"I get it," broke in Timothy the Toucan, bouncing vigorously: "though you were only going to lose one trump trick, you could no longer get rid of your club and diamond losers, and by now Papa had taken two tricks already."

"But surely," objected Oscar, "you could still throw him in with the ♣ K. He would have to lead a heart, and . . ."

"You're doing Papa an injustice," replied the Hog. "Of course I played my ♣ A, but again Papa could see what was coming and he threw his king on the ace. No, there was no longer any way of endplaying him."

"And so . . ." prompted Peregrine.

"And so," continued the Hog, "I endplayed East instead with a diamond, leaving him the choice of leading into dummy's ♣ Q 10 or returning another diamond and presenting me with a ruff and discard."

"But didn't you just tell us," said the Corgi, "that if you had to play against yourself, you would lose a fortune. Does that mean that had you been West, as well as South, you couldn't have made 4 ♠?"

"I wouldn't have given myself the chance," declared the Hog. "I would have broken the contract by . . ."

"But you have just proved that it can't be broken," protested the Owl.

"Not by other Wests," admitted the Hideous Hog; "but then no other West is H.H."

"Like Colin," explained the Hog, "I would have given South a ruff and discard when I was thrown in the first time with the ♡ Q. Then, when I was thrown in the second time with one of my trump honours, I should have given him another ruff and discard. He would have still had a losing club in each hand, of course, so he would throw me in a third time with my second spade honour and I would again play a heart, presenting declarer with yet another ruff and discard."

"What's so clever about that?" asked the Penguin. "Can't he now get rid of that club?"

"Try it," advised H.H. "After three rounds of trumps and three heart ruffs, declarer will be left with one trump facing two losers. He can retain that last trump in either hand, of course, but that will not be much of a consolation."

The Owl hooted softly. "Curious hand," he observed. "South makes his contract by endplaying West three times and West breaks it by three times conceding a ruff and discard."

"Mind you," said the Hog, "Papa didn't play so badly, when all is said and done. Unfortunately for him, he had sealed his fate before trick one by that double of his. Coming on top of the 3 ♡ bid, it pinpointed every card. As West, I shouldn't have had the temerity to double myself as South. But then," sighed H.H., "arrogance has always been Papa's undoing."

The bottle was empty. "Bring me some paper," the Hog called to the barman. It was a purely tactical move. Two books were within easy reach. *Crime and Punishment* was at his elbow, and in the usual way H.H. would have written down the next hand on the fly leaf. But champagne always made him thirsty, and the company needed a reminder.

Chapter 8
THE ACE OF TRUMPS RUNS AWAY

Papa and the Hideous Hog exchanged hostile glances. They had known in their bones that they would cut together, for it wasn't their lucky day. The Stock Exchange was bad. The weather forecast was 'little change' and to add insult to injury, the new barman had mixed them up, mistaking one for the other.

"What are we coming to," snorted the Hog, 'when an imbecile, who addresses me as 'Mr. Papadopoulos', is appointed to a position of responsibility?"

"Did the oaf imagine," spluttered the Greek indignantly, "that even if I were H.H. I would admit it in public?"

"Don't play every hand, I beg of you, Themistocles," pleaded the Hog as he sat down opposite Papa. "I know you need the practice, but spread the risk."

Before Papa had time to put on a look to match his feelings, the cards had been dealt. For a time the game went, as it were, with the service. Whoever was first to speak bid notrumps, and partner gave way stoically. Timothy the Toucan and Karapet Djoulikyan, the Free Armenian, collected their fifties and the odd hundred in silence. They had too much respect for their betters to double them in part-score contracts. Slowly each side crept up to game.

Papa Raises H.H.

Then came this hand:

Dealer West—Game All

Papa
♠ 3 2
♡ J 10 6 5 4
◇ —
♣ 9 8 7 6 5 4

T.T.
♠ K Q 9 8 7
♡ —
◇ K J 9 7 5
♣ K J 10

Karapet
♠ J 10 6 5
♡ A Q
◇ A Q 10 3
♣ Q 3 2

H.H.
♠ A 4
♡ K 9 8 7 3 2
◇ 8 6 4 2
♣ A

West	North	East	South
1 ◇	Pass	1 ♠	Pass
2 ♠	Pass	3 ♡	Pass
3 ♠	Pass	4 ◇	Pass
4 ♠	Pass	4 NT	Pass
5 ♣	Pass	5 ◇	5 ♡
5 ♠	6 ♡	Dble	

Even at the far end of the room the kibitzers could hear the Hog gnash his teeth. Up to Papa's 6 ♡ bid everything had gone according to plan. So long as the hand was to be played in spades, H.H. had no worries. He would lay down the ♣ A and lead a diamond, expecting to find partner with one diamond or none. Then, when he came in with the ♠ A, he would lead a second diamond, giving Papa a ruff and ruffing the club return himself. It promised to be an enjoyable defence.

But just as 4 ♠ was unmakable, so 5 ◇ appeared to be unbeatable, and when it looked as if that would be the final contract, the Hog came in fearlessly with 5 ♥. The sacrifice could hardly be expensive, for in addition to his shortage in diamonds, partner was marked on the bidding with good heart support.

The Toucan's 5 ♠ bid was a pleasant surprise, and H.H. was gloating discreetly when Papa spoilt everything by bursting into 6 ♥.

The Hog snarled.

"With five trumps and a void," began Papa, tabling his hand, "I am entitled, I think . . ."

"Are you suggesting," snapped the Hog, "that I haven't bid your hand fully already? Have you anything over and above my bid? And anyway, since you haven't supported my suit for some years, why should you choose to create a precedent on this particular occasion?"

"Only 1 point," broke in Walter the Walrus in shocked tones.

The Toucan led the ♠ K. The Hog won with the ace, laid down the ♣ A and ruffed a diamond in dummy, then a club in the closed hand. Crossing to the table with a second diamond ruff, he ruffed another club, setting up dummy's ♣ 9 8 7. A third diamond ruff took him back to the table, and now the defence was powerless. In desperation, Karapet ruffed a club with his ♥ Q, but H.H. overruffed, returned to dummy by trumping his last diamond and played another club, throwing on it his ♠ 4.

'I might have known it," sighed the Armenian. "If I pick up a good hand something's bound to go wrong. It's the curse on our family, the evil spell cast on the Djoulikyans. Did I tell you what happened to me on Thursday? I held the . . ."

"Why worry? interrupted the Hog, whose temper had improved markedly. "You made your ace of trumps, didn't you? What more do you want?"

This remark struck him as very funny. Chuckling to himself and grimacing amicably at the kibitzers, he proceeded to write down a hand.

The rubber was over. Papa rose from the table. "I am sure I know your hand," he said, directing at the Hog a look of derision.

"You were South and played brilliantly. Or perhaps you

played brilliantly in some other position. Don't forget to show the hand to the barman."

Winner-on-Loser Play

The deal which the Hog now passed round to us had occurred a week or so earlier in a match between the Friends of Bacchus and the Old Boys of St Swithin's, captained by Walter the Walrus. It wasn't hard to guess what made H.H. think of this hand at this particular juncture.

I had looked in to kibitz the match at the half-way stage and remembered the occasion vividly.

"I am losing £50," the Hog told me gloomily when I asked for the score. "I am playing £5 an I.M.P. and they are only 22 down after 16 hands. I expected the difference at this stage to be 50, at least. It's a lot to make up in a short match."

This was the first board after the interval:

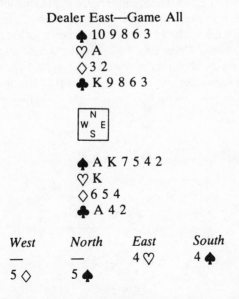

Dealer East—Game All

♠ 10 9 8 6 3
♡ A
◇ 3 2
♣ K 9 8 6 3

```
        N
      W   E
        S
```

♠ A K 7 5 4 2
♡ K
◇ 6 5 4
♣ A 4 2

West	North	East	South
—	—	4 ♡	4 ♠
5 ◇	5 ♠		

The opening lead was the ◇K. East won with the ◇A and led

the ♡ Q, to which West followed with the ♡ 3. To the low trump, which the Hog led from dummy at trick three, East played the jack while West discarded a diamond.

The Hideous Hog sat back, biting fiercely at my cigar as he surveyed the situation.

How could he avoid losing another diamond and a club? The ◇ A was clearly a singleton, since East didn't continue the suit, and he was known to have the ♠ Q J. If he also had three clubs, all was well, for the suit could then be set up without letting West in to cash his diamond. But could East have three clubs? If so, his 4 ♡ opening was based on a seven-card suit, headed by Q J, and an outside ace, six playing tricks all told.

The Hog shook his head. St Swithin's was a good school and no Old Boy was likely to risk a 1,100 penalty so wantonly. East must surely have eight hearts, in which case he would have two clubs only and it might not be possible to keep out West.

With a vicious grunt, the Hog threw the battered remains of my cigar into the fire. Then, suddenly, a light came into his small, beady eyes and the scowl gave way to a euphoric leer. To trick four he led a low club to dummy's king, then another to the ace in the closed hand. When East followed the second time, the Hog uttered a subdued warcry and with exaggerated care placed the ♠ 2 in the centre of the table. This was the deal in full:

```
                  ♠ 10 9 8 6 3
                  ♡ A
                  ◇ 3 2
                  ♣ K 9 8 6 3

        ♠ —                        ♠ Q J
        ♡ 6 5 3          N         ♡ Q J 10 9 8 7 4 2
        ◇ K Q J 10 9 8 7  W   E    ◇ A
        ♣ Q J 10            S      ♣ 7 5

                  ♠ A K 7 5 4 2
                  ♡ K
                  ◇ 6 5 4
                  ♣ A 4 2
```

East registered surprise as he gathered the unexpected trump trick, but now, with only hearts left, he was forced to present declarer with a ruff and discard. The Hog threw his third club and ruffed in dummy, then he trumped a club in his own hand, setting up two long clubs on the table to take care of his two diamonds.

Winning a trump trick, to which they were not entitled, had cost East-West two others, a club and a diamond, which fate had intended them to havé.

Story with an Unhappy Ending

I followed the board to the other room where Walter the Walrus was sitting North. A crowd of kibitzers, sporting St Swithin's gay puce-and-grey ties, were applauding their captain, who had just brought off a finesse.

The first round of bidding followed the same pattern as before, but then events took a different turn:

West	North	East	South
—	—	4 ♡	4♠
5 ◇	5 ♠	Pass	Pass
6 ♡	Dble		

"We'll pick up a bit here," said one puce-and-grey tie to another. "Our side can't make 5 ♠, and theirs won't do so well in a slam with only 19 points to our 21."

"Especially as the ace and king of trumps are missing," rejoined his companion with a chuckle.

South opened the ♠ K and was not unhappy to see declarer ruff in dummy, for now he could take the trump finesse in comfort, losing to the singleton king.

Declarer, however, led a diamond to the closed hand, ruffed his second spade in dummy and continued with the ◇K, on which he discarded a club. The ◇ Q followed.

Walter the Walrus was glad of the opportunity to signal in clubs. "My ace of trumps won't run away," he remarked with a twinkle to a supporter who was breathing encouragement down his neck. Declarer discarded his second club and led dummy's last trump, to bring down the ace and king together.

"That ace of trumps did run away after all," pointed out Colin the Corgi, who was kibitzing for the Friends of Bacchus.

"Yes," agreed one of the younger Old Boys, "the king of trumps would have made anyway, so it's a pity the ace didn't take a trick, too. Would have made all the difference," he added thoughtfully.

Just as the Hideous Hog finished describing the play, with characteristic flourishes and embellishments, Papa sauntered back to our table.

"I have informed the new barman," he said, fixing H.H. with a steely eye, "that he can flatter you as grossly as he pleases. It is no concern of mine. But if he calls me names again, intentionally or otherwise, I shall report him at once to the secretary."

The Hog drew a deep breath. A loud rasping noise came from his throat, but before the first coherent imprecation could emerge, the Greek had turned on his heels and made his exit.

The Hog was well and truly endplayed.

Chapter 9
EXTENDED MENACES

"Do you think there's anything really in all this squeezing business?" asked Timothy the Toucan. "They are always talking about it, I know, but isn't it something that just happens like, well, dropping a singleton king? You can't *make* it happen, can you?"

The Rueful Rabbit reflected as he munched his favourite chocolate almond biscuits.

"Ye-es," he said a little doubtfully, "it just happens, of course, but it happens more often to some than to others. You can read all about it in books, there are menaces and things and . . ."

"Do you mean the Hog?" asked T.T., who was little versed in technical terminology.

"The Hog has more menaces than anyone else," agreed R.R., "which is why people are always throwing their winners away when he's around, but there's more to it than that. The Hog is, er . . ."

"An extended menace?" suggested Colin the Corgi, who had come over to join us for coffee.

"And what's a double squeeze?" asked the Toucan. "They usually double me, as you know, but it's not so much because I throw my winners away, it's rather that I have too many losers and nowhere to throw them, if you see what I mean."

"No, no, you've got it all wrong, Timothy," replied the Rabbit, trying not to sound patronising. "It's quite simple really, though. When some menace makes you throw the wrong card, you've been squeezed, and when, on the same hand, partner also throws the wrong card, there's a double squeeze. It's true that when we play together people double us, but that's only because they expect us to do the wrong thing, anyway, even without menaces. The double is no part of the apparatus as such."

"Maybe," suggested the Corgi pleasantly, "each one of you is a menace to the other, so there's no need for any more menaces."

"And a trump squeeze?" persisted the Toucan in whom the Burgundy at dinner had induced a mellow, enquiring mood. "They say it's harder to execute than others."

"No," the Rabbit shook his head vigorously, "as a rule, it's quite simple. When you have a long suit, you usually make it trumps and that, of course, is when opponents are likely to throw away the odd winner which can make all the difference. I brought off a trump squeeze myself yesterday," added the Rabbit proudly, "against Papa, too."

This was the hand which had given R.R. so much pleasure:

H.H.
♠ K Q 4
♡ Q 6
◇ A J 3
♣ A Q J 8 7

Karapet
♠ 9 7 6 5 3
♡ 10 4
◇ 10 9 4 2
♣ 6 4

```
  N
W   E
  S
```

Papa
♠ J 8
♡ A 7 2
◇ K 8 6
♣ K 10 9 5 3

R.R.
♠ A 10 2
♡ K J 9 8 5 3
◇ Q 7 5
♣ 2

West	North	East	South
—	1 ♣	Pass	1 ♡
Pass	3 NT	Pass	6 ♡
Pass	Pass	Dble	

The bidding was straightforward. Papa doubled on principle and for a club lead, and Karapet duly opened the ♣ 6.

When dummy went down, prospects looked bleak.

"Only 29 points between them," noted Walter the Walrus disapprovingly.

"Not a hope," whispered Oscar the Owl, after walking round the table unobtrusively two or three times. "Every card's wrong."

The Rabbit won the opening lead with the ♣ A and started on the trumps. Papa played low the first time, went up with his ace on the next round and exited with his third trump. R.R. discarded dummy's ◇ 3 and took stock. He was not worried about losers, but the winners seemed to be a little on the thin side. His first thought was to set up a long club, so he crossed to dummy with a spade and led the ♣ Q, which Papa covered with his king. The Rabbit ruffed, led his penultimate trump, and with a crafty look threw on it dummy's ◇ J. Surely, he thought, no one would suspect him of having the queen if he bared dummy's ace. And, anyway, he had no choice, for he couldn't set up dummy's long club if he threw it away, and unfortunately he had no losers in spades. Dummy, in fact, was squeezed.

It didn't seem to matter in which order he played the spades, but being in his hand he started with the ace. As he continued with the ♠ 10 to dummy's queen, this was the position:

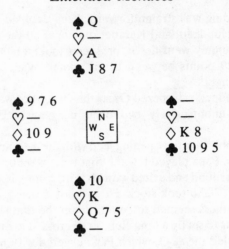

What could Papa throw on that lethal spade? The Rabbit was clearly interested in clubs and might well notice a discard from that suit. Hoping for the best, the Greek bared his ♢K.

The ♣J, on which R.R. threw a diamond, came next, and when Karapet showed out, the Rabbit sighed ruefully. A second later both his ears shot up excitedly, for on his ♢A Papa dropped the king.

"Even the best players are caught napping sometimes," thought R.R., smiling to himself quietly. "My throwing that ♢J took him in completely, but of course he'd never admit it."

"Well played, R.R.," said the Hideous Hog who, up to that point had scowled impartially at all and sundry. "A rash double of yours, Themistocles," he added with a malevolent look at Papa. "Without it, R.R. would doubtless have finessed the ♢J in the ordinary way."

"Was I supposed to know," cried the exasperated Greek, "that without a single revoke, playing repeatedly from the right hand, he would pull all the cards out in the right order to squeeze the life out of me?"

"Just because you threw the wrong card," retorted the Rabbit sharply, "there's no need to be rude."

"It could only happen to me," murmured Karapet sadly. "He

does not always know what the trumps are, yet he brings home a slam on a trump squeeze. It's the curse of the Djoulikyans. Did I tell you what happened to me on Tuesday? I was in . . ."

Post-Mortem

Colin, who had been kibitzing, remembered the hand well and for the Toucan's benefit he pieced it together, card by card, to illustrate the squeeze mechanism.

"But for all that," persisted the Toucan, "it was something that just happened, wasn't it? Papa didn't have to throw that wrong card, did he?"

"True," conceded C.C., "he might have thrown some other wrong card. But what he couldn't do was to throw the right one. That's why it was a squeeze."

The Toucan bounced unsteadily trying to sort things out. "It's all very confusing," he said, "and I know there are lots of other squeezes, for I've seen the complete list, only it was in French or Swiss or something; but the other day, when I had that, er, accident, the Hog called it a progressive squeeze and he seemed to think that I'd done it on purpose . . ."

"No, no," broke in the Rabbit, "we know that you don't do things on purpose, Timothy, and anyway a progressive squeeze is something quite different. For one thing, it is more protracted."

"The pain is long drawn-out" explained the Corgi. "It doesn't only happen, as you put it, but it keeps on happening. As soon as you lose one tooth, the next one starts to hurt. Now take that hand you have just mentioned, the one on which your dummy play was so sensational. . . ." The Toucan winced as Colin wrote down the hands.

Dealer South—E/W Vulnerable and 60

T.T.
♠ A K 3 2
♡ A K J 7
◇ A Q 6
♣ A Q

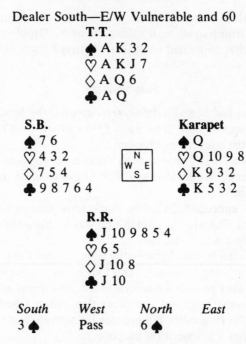

S.B.
♠ 7 6
♡ 4 3 2
◇ 7 5 4
♣ 9 8 7 6 4

Karapet
♠ Q
♡ Q 10 9 8
◇ K 9 3 2
♣ K 5 3 2

R.R.
♠ J 10 9 8 5 4
♡ 6 5
◇ J 10 8
♣ J 10

South	West	North	East
3 ♠	Pass	6 ♠	

The Emeritus Professor of Bio-Sophistry, known as the Secretary Bird, was playing with Karapet, and they were game up and 60 below the line towards the rubber. The Rabbit, who dealt, bid 3 ♠ in desperation and the Toucan promptly raised him to 6 ♠. Much to R.R.'s relief, before anyone could double, the ♠ 7 was gliding across the green baize, and with a jaunty flourish the Toucan began to table his hand. First came the deuce and three of spades, then a splash of honours, three aces, a king and two queens. "You don't expect any trumps from me, of course," chirruped the Toucan with a wink at the kibitzers, "for I have every high card in the pack. Just look, but don't make seven. That's all I ask."

With a heavy heart, the Rabbit flicked the deuce of spades on the seven. Karapet played the queen and, just as R.R. was about to follow himself with the ♠ 4, dummy's last two cards, the ♠ A and ♠ K came belatedly into view.

"Oh!" exclaimed the Rabbit, visibly shaken. The Toucan looked startled. "I was only joking. I wasn't, I mean, I was . . ."

"Take it back," urged Karapet. "That trick wasn't intended for us. We don't want it."

Thrusting out his Adam's apple, the wild tufts of hair over his ears bristling with anger, the Secretary Bird glared at the Armenian. "You happen to have a partner," he hissed. "You have a duty to him and you should know by now that you cannot waive some rules and enforce others. Order and chaos do not blend. That deuce has been played. Your queen has won the trick, and it is your lead."

The Armenian protested, but the Rabbit took all the blame. "I should have looked at dummy first," he said meekly. "I played too quickly."

"A case of mistiming," remarked Colin the Corgi.

It took Karapet a little while to select a card at trick two, for there were twelve that he couldn't possibly play. Eventually he emerged with the deuce of diamonds as the least of many evils. The Rabbit went up with the jack and it held the trick. R.R. was sorely puzzled. If West had the king, why didn't he cover? And if he hadn't, why did East lead the suit? Was he trying to fool him, pretending not to have the king to make sure that he took this particular finesse rather than another which would succeed? He had seen the Hog get away with just such a ruse. Sitting over the A Q, he had led the deuce from K 2, and of course he bamboozled everyone and made his bare king later, and jeered and gloated for the rest of the evening. Was Karapet trying to do something like that?

His nostrils aquiver with excitement, R.R. led a diamond to the ace. Nothing happened, and remembering just in time that someone still had a trump, he played the king of spades.

The moment had come to take the club finesse. If it worked, a successful finesse in hearts would bring home the slam. With eyes half-closed, the Rabbit led the ♣ J.

"You are in dummy," warned the Secretary Bird.

The Rabbit tried to get back to his hand with a trump, but S.B. was too quick for him.

"Kindly play a club," he commanded.

Ruefully the Rabbit led out dummy's ♣ A. Then he settled down to the trumps, bringing about this end position.

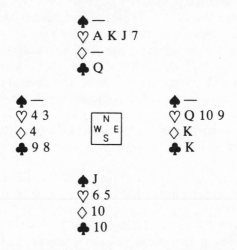

On his last trump the Rabbit threw dummy's ♣ Q and Karapet was in trouble. Forced to choose between unguarding his ♡ Q and letting go one of his kings, the Armenian gave up his ◊ K. The Rabbit spotted it at once and pressed on with the ◊ 10, squeezing Karapet in clubs and hearts. The club situation was ominous, so Karapet parted with a heart. Alas, it had to be the nine and the Rabbit saw it as a signal, proclaiming unmistakably the presence of the queen. R.R. shook his head. If he finessed and failed he might not take another trick, for there were all sorts of clubs out against him and diamonds, too, perhaps. Having recovered so well from the Toucan's illfated jest at trick one, he was ready to concede a paltry 50. The Rabbit nodded approvingly, as if to say 'I couldn't agree with myself more', and promptly cashed two top hearts, felling the queen in the process.

He could hardly believe that Karapet had been so careless as to leave the ♡ Q unguarded, but he didn't like to say anything. These things just happened.

The Armenian turned to S.B. "Not satisfied with endplaying

me at trick one," he said bitterly, "you scorned declarer's help
when he tried to finesse in clubs. No, you had to make him play
from the right hand. You are the only player I have ever met who
can execute a progressive squeeze with a Yarborough."

"A very extended menace," observed Colin the Corgi.

As they recalled the hand, the Toucan, bouncing slowly and a
little unsteadily, tried hard to grasp the mechanics of the squeeze.

"But wouldn't you have made one more trick if you had gone
up with the ace instead of letting Karapet make his bare queen?"

"No, no," explained the Rabbit, "you must always lose a trick
if you are to do any squeezing. It's one of the rules. And the
sooner you do it the better, for it gives defenders more time to
throw the wrong cards. That's why losing the first trick was so
effective. There's a defence to it, though. There always is. When
declarer tries to make you win a trick, to stop him you lose it."

"Perhaps Karapet shouldn't have gone up with his bare
queen," suggested the Corgi amiably.

Rectifying Papa

The Rabbit didn't hear him. There was a faraway look in his eyes
as he searched his memory, trying to reconstruct a hand he had
held against Papa.

"I had to lose two winners to beat the contract, but I can't quite
recall . . ."

Oscar the Owl, who had joined us a few minutes earlier,
recognised the hand at once and proceeded to write it down:

Dealer South—Love All

Karapet
♠ 8 7 5
♡ Q 6
◇ Q J 10 9 8
♣ J 3 2

H.H.
♠ 9 6
♡ K J 9 7 4 3
◇ 6 5 4 3 2
♣ —

```
  N
W   E
  S
```

R.R.
♠ Q J 10 4 2
♡ 10 8 2
◇ 7
♣ Q 10 5 4

Papa
♠ A K 3
♡ A 5
◇ A K
♣ A K 9 8 7 6

South	North
2 ♣	2 ◇
3 NT	

This was the story behind the deal.

The Greek's 3 NT rebid is self-explanatory. Over any other, partner might get the notrumps in first. Then the wrong hand would go down and the wrong player would be dummy.

To the Hog, a lead from his broken heart suit looked distinctly unattractive and, seeing no future in diamonds, he settled on the ♠ 9.

Papa won with the ace, laid down the ♣ A, noting with raised eyebrows the Hog's deuce of diamonds, and continued with the ◇ A and ◇ K. When on the ◇ K the Rabbit threw the ♡ 2, the Greek closed his eyes the better to see the East-West hands. The complete picture quickly came into view. Since the Hog was marked with no fewer than five hearts, his only reason for not leading one must have been a reluctance to play away from the king. That fitted in well with the Rabbit's discard of the deuce on the second round of diamonds.

Reluctantly Papa gave up the idea of setting up the clubs, since in the process he would have to lose five tricks—two clubs and three spades. Yet how could the contract be made without bringing in the clubs?

The solution came to Papa in a flash. At trick five he cashed the ♠ K and, exiting with the three, put the Rabbit on play. With a confident smile he detached the ♡ A, making ready to throw it on the next spade.

At the inquest, held as soon as rigor mortis had set in, the Greek explained his spectacular line of play.

"It didn't matter to me whether R.R. had started with four spades or with five. After taking his winners—he couldn't have more than three—he would have to lead a club, giving me an entry to dummy's diamonds, or else a heart, and again dummy would have an entry—so long as my ♡ A didn't stand in the way. All I had to do was to get rid of that ace before a heart was led. H.H. would win the fourth trick for the defence with his king, but with red cards only left, he couldn't avoid giving me access to dummy."

Such was Papa's pretty plan, and it would have surely succeeded but for an unforeseeable move by the Rabbit. Instead of cashing his two good spades, he switched to a heart. Papa was helpless. He played low, but as he rightly suspected, the Hog had the king and he promptly returned a heart, locking Papa in his hand.

Papa looked reproachfully at the Rabbit. "I know it was unpremeditated, but why," he asked him, "did you not cash those two splendid spades while you had the chance? Why did you switch to a heart?"

"Because," replied R.R. with dignity, "I am not quite as ignorant as you seem to think. You wanted me to cash my spades to rectify the count and let you squeeze H.H. Well, I . . ."

"What squeeze?" cried Papa in exasperation. "Have you discovered a fifth suit or was H.H. going to be squeezed out of his void in clubs?"

"Yes," said the Rabbit ruefully as Oscar recalled Papa's remarks, "despite all the practice he's had, Themistocles isn't a good loser. He can take it when H.H. breaks up his squeezes, but if I do it he becomes bitter and sarcastic."

Chapter 10
IN SEARCH OF LOSERS

Bela Gulash was not his real name. He had only assumed it so as to pass unnoticed among the senior civil servants in Whitehall with whom his work brought him so frequently into contact. Few outside the inner Cabinet knew his true identity. Few outside the enemy's secret service knew the nature of the mysterious project for reintegrating the atom on which he was working at Aix-on-Wye. No newspaper in England, and only two abroad, had been permitted to photograph the entrance to his laboratory, cunningly concealed behind the façade of the sleepy village betting shop.

"Do, please, make us up," begged the Rueful Rabbit. "I must leave early this afternoon and if we don't start now, I may not get a game at all."

"It wouldn't really be fair to my partner," protested the great physicist. "I can't see at all well without my reading glasses, and unfortunately, I left them behind in my car. I, er, really . . ."

"We'll wait for you while you get them," suggested the Rabbit eagerly. "We'll cut and deal and sort our cards and . . ."

Gulash shook his head. "I only wish," he said wistfully "that I knew where I left my car. One can't remember everything, you know, and I have an uncomfortable feeling that I may have come up by taxi. Still, if you insist . . . I'll . . . er. . ." His voice trailed off as he cut a card drawing as his partner the Emeritus Professor of Bio-Sophistry, better known to us all as the Secretary Bird.

The Rabbit cut Walter the Walrus, the greatest points specialist in the club, if not in Western Europe.

I had wandered into the room a few minutes earlier, and after walking round the table to see all four hands, I settled in a seat between the Rabbit and the nuclear wizard. Walter the Walrus dealt:

Dealer North—Love All
W.W.
♠ Q J 2
♡ 7 6 5 4
◇ J 2
♣ A K J 9

Bela Gulash
♠ —
♡ J 10 9 8
◇ A K Q 10 7
♣ Q 10 3 2

```
  N
W   E
  S
```

S.B.
♠ 10 9 8 7 6 5 4
♡ —
◇ 5
♣ 8 7 6 5 4

R.R.
♠ A K 3
♡ A K Q 3 2
◇ 9 8 6 4 3
♣ —

West	North	East	South
—	1 ♣	3 ♠	3 NT
Dble			

Bela led the ◇ K, then the ◇ Q on which his partner, the
Secretary Bird, threw a small spade. The ♡ J followed. When
R.R. produced the ace, there was a strange and ominous rumble
to his left. For a moment I thought I was about to witness the
reintegration of the atom. But that was still to come. The dis-
quieting noise, it transpired, was due to Bela's discovery that he
had mistaken the ♡ J for the ◇ J.

"Please take it back," cried the Rabbit.

"Wouldn't dream of it," replied Gulash vehemently.

"It was so sporting of you to make us up after mislaying your
glasses" persisted R.R. "I couldn't possibly take advantage . . . I
mean. . .I now have ten tricks on top. . .I couldn't. . .wouldn't. . ."

"No, no, I had the first five tricks to make, which is why I
doubled, of course; but one must pay for one's carelessness and I
have no doubt that my partner feels as I do."

There was an ugly hiss from the Secretary Bird, but Gulash did not seem to hear it.

The Rabbit's Grand Design

It was at this point that the Rabbit conceived the Machiavellian scheme of throwing the contract away deliberately. At first his chances did not seem too good. He could see three inescapable spade tricks, five hearts, as he thought, and two top clubs. With so many tricks about, it was not going to be easy to lose three more, but he would do his best.

So far he had lost two tricks to the king and queen of diamonds, and he had captured the ♡ J with the ace. With his mind set loftily on *felo de se*, R.R. led out the king and queen of hearts, without bothering to note who followed or for how long. Then—and this was the key to his play—he led the ace and king of spades, throwing on them dummy's queen and jack. Now he could afford to sit back happily.

The Emeritus Professor of Bio-Sophistry blinked. He had no interest in the hand, since he could not possibly win a trick, but he discarded with care if only to protect partner. He had parted with a spade on the second diamond and he threw two more, then a club, on the three top hearts.

To find himself thrown in suddenly with a spade came as a complete surprise, and he did the obvious thing by cashing his fourth and last spade while he had the chance.

The atom man, meanwhile, was in excruciating pain, having to find four discards on those spades. He could afford to let go three diamonds, since R.R. had no entry left to his hand. But what could he spare for that fourth, intolerable spade? The position at this juncture was:

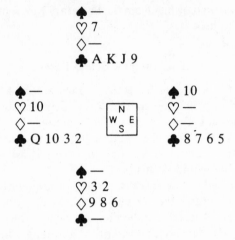

```
              ♠ —
              ♡ 7
              ◇ —
              ♣ A K J 9

   ♠ —                        ♠ 10
   ♡ 10          N            ♡ —
   ◇ —        W     E         ◇ —
   ♣ Q 10 3 2    S            ♣ 8 7 6 5

              ♠ —
              ♡ 3 2
              ◇ 9 8 6
              ♣ —
```

Unhappily, Gulash parted with a club, keeping the ♡ 10. The Rabbit wasn't even looking. He had managed to shed one of his unwanted ten winners by creating a spade loser and he was now in a position to get rid of another by discarding dummy's heart, which looked to him every inch a trick.

Having run out of spades, the Secretary Bird looked in vain for something to lead that would not be a club. Nothing, alas, was available and, despite his best endeavours, R.R. found himself with nine inescapable tricks.

To this day, the Rueful Rabbit doesn't know what made the Emeritus Professor lead a club into dummy's tenace or why Gulash had discarded so unwisely on the spades. He had an uneasy feeling that, perhaps, the scientist had guessed his grand design and was throwing the contract back at him deliberately.

"Curious hand," observed Oscar the Owl, our Senior Kibitzer. "If Mr Gulash had led another diamond, as was his intention, declarer could have made his contract by setting up a diamond for his ninth trick. That heart switch, if a little inadvertent, produced the only defence to tie declarer down to his eight top tricks. A lucky masterstroke, so to speak."

Suddenly there came a choking sound from the corner of the room. The Hideous Hog, who had just entered, was trying to make an important pronouncement and, at the same time, to swallow a handful of chocolate truffles. By the time all but two had been despatched, he was able to articulate audibly.

"Don't blame our poor friend," he pleaded. "After all, he doesn't usually play his dummy with malice aforethought and if he made the maximum this time, it was only because he was trying so hard to make a minimum. Ha! ha!"

"But . . ." began Oscar.

"No, no, you're quite wrong, I assure you," went on H.H. "The interesting point about the hand is that there is no way of losing the contract. It's foolproof. Better still, as you've just seen, it's Rabbit-proof."

The Hog emptied a glass—I can't recall whose it was—and continued: "All declarer need do after the heart switch is to play the ace and king of spades. Immediately, West is exposed to a three-suit squeeze. He can part with a club, but his next discard spells his doom. If he lets go a heart, all the hearts are good. If he throws a diamond, declarer has still time to set one up.

"Even after playing the three top hearts," pursued H.H., "declarer cannot help himself. He's done his best to lose the contract, but it's no good. West must still find three discards on the spades. If he lets go a club and two diamonds, he's thrown in with a heart and, after cashing his last diamond, he must lead a club away from his queen."

"Yes, yes," broke in someone, "but as the play went, East need not have cashed that last spade. It was a suicide squeeze and . . ."

"Supremely unimportant," declared the Hog with a sweeping gesture. "If the Professor switches to a club at once, without cashing his last spade, declarer wins in dummy and throws West in with the last heart, compelling him to lead another club into the tenace on the table.

"So you see," concluded the Hog, "declarer is helpless. He cannot avoid executing a squeeze or an endplay. He may not know what coup he is performing, but perform it he must."

The hand made a deep impression on the Rabbit, and he

brought it up again the next day when I joined him for lunch at the Unicorn.

As I came up to the table, R.R. had just settled the particulars of his salad. Monsieur Merle, the head waiter, had departed. The Rabbit, who didn't notice it, was saying: "... and a little avocado, thinly sliced, to blend with the tarragon leaves and, perhaps ..."

Suddenly, aware of my presence, he stopped in his tracks and blushed deeply.

"Forgive me," he apologised. "I'm a little distrait this morning. I've been thinking about that hand last night when I tried so hard to lose the contract and there was no way of doing it.

"Have you considered," he went on, "that it's sometimes more difficult to lose tricks than to win them? You remember that extraordinary hand I had not long ago against the American? Well . . ."

May the Worst Man Win

Over a carafe of chilled Tavel and the St-Estèphe which followed, we recalled the strange circumstances of a deal which had come up a fortnight earlier.

The Toucan and an American visitor, who was making his first appearance at the Griffins, were opposed to the Rabbit and the Chimp. As I joined the kibitzers who had gathered around them, R.R. was picking up his cards.

Dealer West—Love All

American
♠ A J 4 3 2
♡ —
♢ A 8 7 6
♣ K 9 8 5

R.R.
♠ 9 6
♡ J 9 7 6 5
♢ Q 5 3
♣ 7 6 4

Ch.Ch.
♠ K Q 10 8 7
♡ 3 2
♢ J 10 9
♣ Q J 10

T.T.
♠ 5
♡ A K Q 10 8 4
♢ K 4 2
♣ A 3 2

West	North	East	South
Pass	1 ♠	Pass	3 ♡
Pass	3 ♠	Pass	4 ♡
Pass	Pass	Dble	Pass
Pass	Redble		

Charlie the Chimp doubled because he knew the Toucan and didn't like the bidding. The American redoubled because he didn't know the Toucan and didn't like the Chimp. Also it was a matter of common courtesy.

The Rabbit led the ♠ 9. After one look at dummy, the Toucan bounced excitedly in his chair for he was pretty confident of an overtrick. On his double the Chimp was surely marked with the hearts, so he would make all his trumps, ruffing spades in the closed hand, overruffing, if need be, and cash his tops in the side-suits as he went along.

Winning the first trick with dummy's ♠ A, the Toucan ruffed a spade, laid down the ♣ A, crossed to the ♣ K and led another spade, all set to ruff again. Already he had detached the ♡ 8 when there occurred an unfortunate diversion.

The Rabbit, a lifelong abstainer from nonalcoholic beverages, had been told that in the States they use water for drinking and put ice in it to kill the taste. As a gesture of hospitality he had invited the American to join him in a glass of water. Wincing at the unaccustomed sensation, he hastened to put down his glass and in the process dropped his cards on the table. All but the ♡ J 9 7 came down face upward.

"Oh dear," exclaimed the Rabbit. "I'm exposed, I mean . . ."

"Do you want to know the Law?" broke in the Secretary Bird eagerly. "It is under section 50, page 27 and says . . ."

"Please stop," cried the Toucan. "I wouldn't dream of taking advantage of an accident."

"You must," insisted the Rabbit. "It was entirely my fault."

"Not at all," protested the Toucan. "How could you guess that they'd slip ice into it? The sudden shock would upset anyone. Please pick up those cards."

"They're exposed," repeated the Rabbit firmly.

"I won't call them," declared the Toucan.

"Then I'll select them myself—to your advantage."

"Two can play at that game," countered the Toucan defiantly.

"Perhaps we ought to wash the hand out," suggested the Chimp, who was beginning to regret his double. No one paid attention to him.

Replacing the ♡ 8, the Toucan ruffed dummy's spade flamboyantly with the ace.

In the same movement the Rabbit underruffed with the ♡ 6. The Toucan laid down the ◇ K. Smiling, the Rabbit threw his queen. Timothy crossed to the ◇ A and led another spade, ruffing ostentatiously with the king. Once more R.R. underruffed. With the ◇ 5 and ♣ 7 still exposed, this was the five-card ending:

♠ J
♡ —
◇ 8 7
♣ 9 8

♠ —
♡ J 9 7
◇ 5
♣ 7

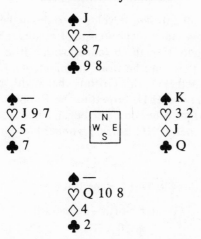

♠ K
♡ 3 2
◇ J
♣ Q

♠ —
♡ Q 10 8
◇ 4
♣ 2

The Toucan exited with the ◇4, and with the queen out of the way, the trick went to the Chimp's jack. Back came a trump, T.T.'s eight losing to the nine. Now the ♣ 7, the last of the exposed cards, once more put Charlie on play. The lead through the closed hand ensured for the defence the fourth, decisive trick.

"May the worst man win," murmured Colin the Corgi softly.

"This, er, variation of the game is new to me," said the American. "We don't have it in the States, but I must admit that the play by both parties has been of the highest order."

"True," agreed the Hog, "but that's only because being so noble-minded, they were trying to play badly." And he proceeded to explain that without the two underruffs the Rabbit's last five cards would have all been trumps. He would have had to ruff declarer's third diamond and return a trump into the Q 10 8. The Toucan would have exited with his club loser, and again R.R. would have been compelled to ruff and lead away from his J 9 into T.T.'s trump tenace. Instead of going one down, he would have made an overtrick.

"Isn't it curious," I said to the Hog, when we discussed the hand later, "that the Rabbit seems to find it just as hard to lose tricks as to make them?"

"Not as curious as it seems," replied H.H. "That Rabbit has

what one may call anti-flair developed to the highest degree, so he usually achieves the exact opposite of whatever he intends."

After pausing for thought, he added with a grin: "I'll devise a neat little test. I am sure he won't let me down."

We dined together at the Griffins that night, and after the *ortolans à la Carème* H.H. turned to the Rabbit.

"I had a hand the other day," he began amiably, scribbling on the back of the menu. "Here it is. I wonder how you would play it."

A Test for the Rabbit

Dealer North—Game All

♠ 10 4 3
♡ A Q 8 6
◇ A Q 10 8
♣ A 3

```
  N
W   E
  S
```

♠ A 9 6
♡ K 7 5 4 3
◇ 5 4 3
♣ Q 4

West	North	East	South
—	1 NT	2 ◇	2 ♡
2 ♠	3 ♡	Pass	4 ♡
Lead: ♠ K			

The Rabbit looked startled. He wasn't accustomed to being consulted, least of all by the Hog.

"There's no catch," added H.H. reassuringly. "It's just a matter of style. Remember the bidding? West leads the ♠ K, to which East follows with the deuce. Go on from there."

His suspicions partly allayed, the Rabbit pondered.

"Trumps break 2–2," said H.H. encouragingly.

"Clearly," soliloquised the Rabbit, "the diamond honours are over dummy, so there's no point in finessing. No, after drawing trumps I'll throw West in with a spade. Maybe he has no diamond and will have to lead a club away from his king."

"But if West has the ♣ K," objected H.H., "East is left with at best 6 points for his vulnerable overcall."

"All right, then," came back the Rabbit, changing course, "when West switches to a club I go up with the ace and play another, endplaying East."

"He'll have to give you a ruff and discard or lead a diamond. True enough, but that will still leave you with a diamond loser, won't it?" pointed out H.H.

"If every card is wrong," retorted the Rabbit, "I'll be doing well to go only one down. Silly hand!"

"And yet," went on H.H., "you can't lose it."

"What do you mean, I can't lose it?" cried the exasperated Rabbit. "I've just done it, haven't I?"

"That's only because you were trying not to," countered the Hog. "Now, just to please me, try to lose it. I assure you that you won't succeed."

"Nonsense!" exclaimed the Rabbit.

The Hog put on his most engaging leer.

"Very well," said the Rabbit, determined to teach the Hog a lesson. "I accept the challenge and we'll have a magnum on the result. How about it?"

H.H. agreed with alacrity.

"Where am I?" asked the Rabbit.

"In your hand or in dummy," said the Hog, "whichever you prefer. You've drawn trumps in two rounds and you can do anything you like—so long, that is, as you try to lose the contract."

"I cash the ♣ A to set up their king," said the defiant R.R.; "then I lead the ◇ Q."

The Hog beamed with pleasure as he congratulated the Rabbit. "You are home and dry. Nothing can now rob you of the contract. Well done."

"I've lost two tricks already and I still have a diamond and two spades to lose," rejoined the Rabbit.

"A diamond perhaps," agreed the Hog, "but the spades will disappear, vanish into thin air as they say. When East comes in with his ◇ K, he'll give you a ruff and discard or lead another diamond. You'll cash the ◇ A and continue with dummy's last diamond, throwing a spade. Now a club from East—or another diamond—will allow you to get rid of your last spade. A simple ruff and discard situation."

"And why, may I ask," broke in the Rabbit, "should East do any such thing? Why shouldn't he return a spade?"

"Because he cannot have one," explained the Hog. "His deuce of spades at trick one should have told you the whole story. Consider. With four spades West wouldn't have bid 2 ♠ over your 2 ♡, would he? And if he had five East would have had a doubleton, so he would have signalled."

"He might have wanted a switch," objected the Rabbit.

The Hog shook his head. "That king could have been from A K, in which case East would want him to continue. No, that deuce could only be a singleton, and it should have pinpointed every card."

The Hog filled in the other hands before he called the sommelier:

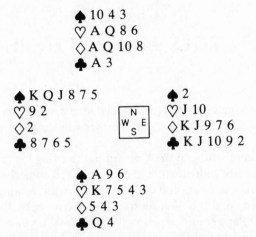

♠ 10 4 3
♡ A Q 8 6
◇ A Q 10 8
♣ A 3

♠ K Q J 8 7 5
♡ 9 2
◇ 2
♣ 8 7 6 5

♠ 2
♡ J 10
◇ K J 9 7 6
♣ K J 10 9 2

♠ A 9 6
♡ K 7 5 4 3
◇ 5 4 3
♣ Q 4

Plunged deep in thought, the Rabbit didn't see him. He was speaking to himself under his breath: "If I try to make the contract I lose it. If I try to lose it I make it. There must be a moral in it somewhere. Perhaps I try too hard with all those endplays and things. Yes, that's it. I'm a natural player, and I should stick to my own style."

"That magnum . . ." murmured H.H.

"I'm natural," said R.R. in a loud voice, coming out of his reverie.

"Yes, sir," said the sommelier.

Chapter 11
TOPS AND BOTTOMS

For once the Hideous Hog saw eye to eye with Papa the Greek. Both had been wronged, and neither was disposed to forget or forgive.

We were sitting in the Unicorn bar, waiting for the results of the monthly Individual, and everyone had something bitter to say about the twists and quirks of matchpoint scoring. The Hog admitted sombrely that he had probably won by the slimmest margin. Papa confided privately that he was no more than a top or two in front of the rest. Everyone had fixed him. The worst players in the room—and there were hardly any others—had performed superbly against him. Then, the moment they faced him, they relapsed into lunacy laced liberally with masochism. Even his friend, Karapet, had let him down badly.

"No, no," broke in the Free Armenian at this point in Papa's lamentations, "it was your fault. Ask anyone. Show them the hand." As he spoke Karapet Djoulikyan passed round this diagram:

Papa	Karapet
♠ 4 3	♠ A K 2
♡ A Q 9 8 7 6	♡ 5 4 3
◇ K 10 4	◇ A J 9 5 2
♣ A 4	♣ 3 2

"The Rueful Rabbit, who was sitting North," explained the Armenian, "opened the ♣ Q against Papa's 4 ♡. How should he have played the hand?"

"You missed a top?" enquired the Hog in surprise.

Ignoring him, Papa turned to Oscar the Owl. "What would you do?" he asked.

O.O. blinked slowly, waiting hopefully for ideas. None

intruded, and at last he said: "I lay down the ace of hearts. Then, if the king doesn't drop, I cross to dummy with a spade to lead another heart. It's a safety play. . ."

"But if North has the ♡ K J x," cut in Papa crisply, "you lose two trumps and a club. Then you misguess the diamond and go down."

"If everything is wrong," retorted the Owl testily, "and if one isn't allowed to find the ◇Q either, the contract's unmakable, so what do you expect me to do?"

"To make it, of course, as I did," declared Papa proudly. "After laying down the ace of hearts, at trick two, you lead out the ace and king of spades and ruff a spade. Then you exit with a club—and you don't care who wins or what happens next. If a trump is led—by either defender—you lose one trump only. A diamond finds the queen for you, and anything else gives you a ruff and discard. That's perfect technique and defenders have no answer to it," concluded the Greek triumphantly.

"Yes," said Karapet sadly, "it was one of my coldest bottoms. Every other declarer in the room made thirteen tricks. Only my Papa confined himself to eleven."

"And only your Papa could do it," remarked the Hog good-humouredly. "I remember the hand well. The ♡ K x are under the A Q and the ◇Q is bare. Ha! ha!"

"That's duplicate for you," cried Papa indignantly. "The only declarer in the room to play correctly gets a bottom."

Karapet sighed deeply. "You forget that you were my partner, Papa," he said reproachfully. "You know that I am the unluckiest player north of the Equator—and on the southern side, too, for that matter. Every card was bound to be wrong—which means, at duplicate, that it would be right. Without a thought for me, you did nothing to guard against good fortune."

The Owl hooted softly. "It is sometimes better," he murmured, "to play badly than to play too well. At least if things go wrong, you are in good company."

A Surfeit of Tricks

"How did you fare on this one?" asked the Hideous Hog, thrusting a hand at the Greek:

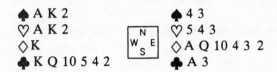

```
♠ A K 2              ♠ 4 3
♡ A K 2              ♡ 5 4 3
◇ K                  ◇ A Q 10 4 3 2
♣ K Q 10 5 4 2       ♣ A 3
```

"One of my early boards," replied Papa without much interest. "I was on 6 NT like everyone else, I suppose, so I put it down, tentatively, as an average."

"Average!" repeated the Hog scornfully. "You mean, no doubt, that you botched it up, Themistocles. How do *you* play it, Oscar? North leads the ♠ Q against your 6 NT."

The Owl pondered. "I seem to have sixteen tricks," he said at last. "If, however, the diamonds are 4–2 and the jack doesn't come down, I can only make thirteen. What's the problem?"

"Play on," insisted the Hog.

Oscar went through the motions: "At trick two, the ◇K. Then a club to the ace and the ace and queen of diamonds. Someone shows out?"

"North," answered H.H. laconically.

"I play on the clubs," went on O.O.

"North has a singleton," said the Hog. "South comes in with the ♣ J and cashes the ◇ J. One down. Bad luck, Oscar."

"Console yourself," said Papa reassuringly. "All the Wests must have suffered the same misfortune."

"Except one," snapped the Hideous Hog. "For my part, I don't hold with misfortune. After taking the ◇ K at trick two, I *ducked* a club and as soon as South followed, I spread my cards. Nothing could go wrong. Papa himself couldn't fail. . ."

"How absurd!" interrupted the Greek vehemently. "Every declarer in the room makes thirteen tricks while you think up a safety play for twelve. A few minutes ago you were ridiculing safety plays at duplicate. Now you turn a somersault. Why? I'll tell you. Because it so happens that both minors broke badly, quite against the odds, mind you, but all your life, my dear H.H., you have been a dedicated and unscrupulous result merchant."

"Certainly," replied H.H., "when the results bear out my expectations, I approve of them, and they usually conform.

"On that last hand, on which you fixed poor Karapet, every West was bound to be in 4 ♡, so you certainly couldn't afford any highfalutin safety plays. This time, as Oscar pointed out, it's long odds on making thirteen tricks and the strongest pairs would, therefore, bid the grand slam. Since you stopped in six, just as I did, you couldn't avoid an indifferent result by making thirteen tricks. Your only hope of a really good score was a bad break in both minors. Then the good bidders, who reached the grand slam, would go down, while the good cardplayers, whose partners bid badly and stayed in a small one, would gather the matchpoints."

A Book Double

"Yes, that was a co-top for you, H.H.," said S.B., the Emeritus Professor of Bio-Sophistry, "but I did even better the other way. We got them one down doubled in 7 ♣. It was our last board and I could see that our 200 was a cold top."

"Doubled? Who? Why? How? . . ." Sceptical eyebrows went up round the table.

"My partner was the Rabbit," explained the Secretary Bird. "Sitting South with J x x x in both minors, he made what he described as a book double . . ."

"Book double? Who could have written such a crazy book?" I asked incredulously.

"You did, I believe," replied S.B. "The idea. . .er, your idea, to be precise, is that no one but a lunatic would double a grand slam with a finessible trump honour. So the double protects the honour. It's an insurance that declarer won't guess right, since he won't suspect a lunatic. . ."

R.R. Savages Papa

"Talking of lunatics reminds me of another board," broke in the Hog. "Papa has my entire sympathy in being savaged by that Rabbit when he had played so well—just as I had played myself, in fact. Ha! ha!"

This was the board of which the recollection gave H.H. so much pleasurable amusement:

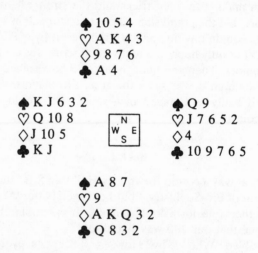

```
                    ♠ 10 5 4
                    ♡ A K 4 3
                    ◇ 9 8 7 6
                    ♣ A 4

   ♠ K J 6 3 2                    ♠ Q 9
   ♡ Q 10 8           N           ♡ J 7 6 5 2
   ◇ J 10 5        W     E        ◇ 4
   ♣ K J             S            ♣ 10 9 7 6 5

                    ♠ A 8 7
                    ♡ 9
                    ◇ A K Q 3 2
                    ♣ Q 8 3 2
```

At most tables the bidding had followed this pattern:

South	North
1 ◇	1 ♡
2 ♣	3 ◇
3 NT	

The contract was only made twice. Every West opened a spade, and most Souths held up the Ace till the third round. Then they embarked on the diamonds and discovered that the suit was blocked in dummy. Result: one down.

Walter the Walrus was the first declarer to overcome the bad diamond break. Coming in with the ace of spades, after holding it up twice, he played one round of diamonds, and when all followed he spread his hand.

"I will not waste your time, gentlemen," he said. "I'll take five diamonds, two hearts and the two black aces."

All agreed. It was as plain as a pikestaff.

"Several declarers went down!" exclaimed West incredulously, opening the travelling scoresheet. "Seems impossible."

The only other successful declarer was H.H. He won the second spade and played back the suit. West pounced on it avidly and took his winners. The Hog gratefully discarded one of dummy's diamonds, unblocking the suit and releasing his ninth trick.

Papa had the board against the Rabbit, sitting West, and Timothy Toucan.

Like the Hog, Papa won the second round of spades and returned another.

Munching furiously at a chocolate almond biscuit, R.R. returned the ◇10. After that there was no play for the contract.

"Why didn't you cash your spades?" asked Papa. "I suppose you were afraid of a crossruff!"

"There's no need to be sarcastic," replied the Rabbit with hauteur. "I knew perfectly well what you were doing. You only had eight tricks, and so you looked to a suicide squeeze for the ninth. If I cashed my spades, as you wanted me to do, I would have nothing to throw on your fourth diamond, and I'd be squeezed in hearts and clubs. I've learned quite a bit about squeezes lately, you know, and I wasn't going to commit *felo de se* to please anyone. Besides, what was the hurry? I could always cash my spades later if I wanted to, couldn't I? I mean if. . ."

As the Rabbit drooled on, the Greek was bemoaning his fate: "He's obsessed with squeezes. He sees them everywhere. He doesn't even know what suicide he isn't committing, and I have to pay for it. Just my luck."

"Your luck!" cried the outraged Karapet, who was waiting to collect the board. "You talk of luck to me! Why, you don't know what bad luck is. Did I tell you . . . ?"

"Move for round seven," called the Tournament Director.

Co-Top or Co-Bottom

The players consulted the direction card and rose. The Rabbit wandered all round the room looking for his partner before discovering that he was due to play with Karapet at the same table.

"Fortune's favourite and the son of sorrow," murmured Colin the Corgi. "I wonder who will prevail."

"It's so confusing not moving," complained the Rabbit testily. "Now we'll have to hurry and if we are late we'll be fined and if. . ." His voice trailed off as he picked up the cards:

Dealer West—Love All

```
        ♠ 10 9 2
        ♡ A 10 3 2
        ◇ 9
        ♣ J 10 9 8 7

            N
        W       E
            S

        ♠ K Q J
        ♡ K Q J
        ◇ K J 10 8 5
        ♣ A K
```

West	North	East	South
1 ♠	Pass	Pass	Dble
Pass	2 ♣	Pass	3 NT

West led the ♠ 5 to East's ♠ 8 and Karapet's king. Allowing for another spade, the Armenian could see eight certain tricks. Where should he look for the ninth?

He couldn't set up the clubs and get back to enjoy them with only one entry in dummy, and if he lost the lead twice in diamonds, opponents would have time to clear their spades.

As he wondered on which sharp horn of the dilemma he should come to rest, the Rabbit was looking anxiously round the room.

"They've nearly all finished," he warned Karapet. "We shall be fined. I don't want to rush you, but. . ."

Spurred on by a sense of urgency, Karapet had a sudden burst of inspiration. A blaze of inner light illumined every card and, with a dramatic gesture worthy of Papa, he tabled his hand.

"Since time presses," he announced, "I won't go through all the motions. I'll just explain how I propose to make the contract regardless of the distribution.

"I'll start with the ♣ A K and follow with four rounds of hearts, overtaking and discarding my ♠ Q on the ♡ 10. Next I'll lead the ♣ J and throw on it my ♠ J, setting up the clubs.

"If you clear the spades," he went on, turning to West, "you will let me into dummy with the ♠ 10. And if you don't, I'll have time to establish my diamonds. Either way, no matter who has what, I shall make nine tricks, ten if. . ."

"My ♣ Q drops," broke in West.

"My ◇ Q is bare," echoed East.

This was the deal:

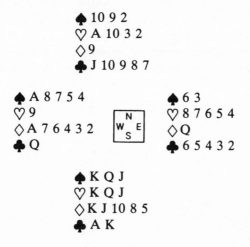

```
                ♠ 10 9 2
                ♡ A 10 3 2
                ◇ 9
                ♣ J 10 9 8 7

    ♠ A 8 7 5 4              ♠ 6 3
    ♡ 9           N          ♡ 8 7 6 5 4
    ◇ A 7 6 4 3 2  W   E     ◇ Q
    ♣ Q           S          ♣ 6 5 4 3 2

                ♠ K Q J
                ♡ K Q J
                ◇ K J 10 8 5
                ♣ A K
```

"It was considerate of you to table your hand and save time," said West, "and since you really couldn't avoid making eleven tricks we will, of course, concede them, though strictly speaking. . ." He left the sentence unfinished.

Karapet looked crestfallen. He had shown true brilliance, and all to no purpose. Fate, through an infernally lucky distribution, had cheated him of his finest play.

"Cheer up," said the Rabbit, unfolding the travelling slip, "you were going to play very well. Isn't that all that matters? And, anyway, it's the same result everywhere. So it's a co-top. No one has made more tricks than you have."

"A co-bottom," corrected Karapet sombrely. "No one made fewer."

"Honours even, I think," observed the Corgi.

South Raises West

The last round brought together the Rueful Rabbit and Walter the Walrus. Opposing them were Timothy the Toucan and the Secretary Bird.

T.T. dealt and bid 1♠. Heaving his huge bulk from side to side, the Walrus meditated deeply, looked at the vulnerability and repeated slowly, "One spade." Then, setting down his coffee cup, he doubled. The clatter of his spoon as it fell to the floor muted the sound, leaving the Rabbit, confused as ever, with the impression that W.W. had opened the bidding with 1♠:

Dealer West—N/S Vulnerable

W.W.
♠ 2
♡ A Q 3 2
◇ A 9 3 2
♣ A Q 3 2

T.T.
♠ A K J 10
♡ K J
◇ Q J 8
♣ K J 10 9

	N	
W		E
	S	

S.B.
♠ 8 7 6
♡ 10 9 8 7
◇ 7 6 5
♣ 8 7 6

R.R.
♠ Q 9 5 4 3
♡ 6 5 4
◇ K 10 4
♣ 5 4

West	North	East	South
1 ♣	Dble	Pass	2 ♠
Pass	3 ♠	Pass	4 ♠
Dble	Redble		

What was to the Rabbit a simple raise was a strength-showing, game-going bid to the Walrus. If R.R. had the right cards, even a slam wasn't to be ruled out. But what in? The book bid in such situations is 3 ♠ and W.W., who read books, even if he didn't always understand what he read, duly bid 3 ♠.

The Rabbit knew that he should pass, but he was in a venture-some mood and it needed only one more for game, so he chanced his arm.

A growl from the Walrus registered disapproval. Why did that Rabbit pass the buck? Why couldn't he choose his own suit?

Before the Walrus could think of anything to say, the Toucan's providential double saved him from his predicament. Now, without further ado, the Rabbit would have to place the contract. To avoid any possible misunderstanding and make assurance doubly sure, the Walrus redoubled.

With a guilty look for he felt he owed his partner a king, if not an ace, the Rabbit passed and he was about to table his hand when the Toucan led the ♠ K.

"Lead out of turn, I think," he began. He was soon put right. All speaking at once, as is usual on such occasions, the situation was explained to him.

"What, me in game? I mean, I in spades? Redouble? I, er, we . . ." dithered the Rabbit.

"Let's wash the hand out," suggested the Toucan. "An average would. . ."

He got no further. "Certainly not!" cried the Secretary Bird. "The laws are there to be observed, not to be flouted, and I would remind you that section 21 of Part V states explicitly: 'A player has no recourse if he has made a call on the basis of a misunderstanding.' Of course, if you wish, you may call the tournament director. He will repeat what I have just said."

"No, no," protested R.R. "I don't want to flout or call anyone. Sorry, Walter. With all this noise around, it isn't easy to concentrate. Still, I don't suppose that one more bottom will make all that difference. And don't you worry, Timothy."

Reluctantly the Toucan gathered the trick. No continuation looked attractive, and after detaching first one card, then another, he finally settled on the ◇ Q as the least dangerous.

The Rabbit won in his hand, finessed a club and ruffed a club. He ran the ◇ 10, led another diamond to the ace and ruffed dummy's last club. Then he took the heart finesse and cashed the ace, leaving this position:

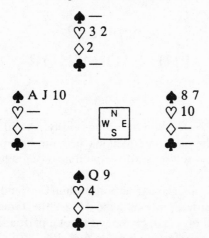

```
              ♠ —
              ♡ 3 2
              ◇ 2
              ♣ —

♠ A J 10                    ♠ 8 7
♡ —          N             ♡ 10
◇ —       W     E          ◇ —
♣ —          S             ♣ —

              ♠ Q 9
              ♡ 4
              ◇ —
              ♣ —
```

With nine tricks stacked neatly in front of him, an unhoped-for result, the Rabbit sighed with relief. To the eleventh trick he led the ◇ 2 and when S.B. ruffed, the Rabbit discarded his ♡ 4, a loser-on-loser play, as he explained later.

For some reason which wasn't apparent to him, the Toucan overruffed and, with the ♠ A J only left, was obliged to concede a trick to the Rabbit's ♠ Q.

"What a pity, Professor," said Colin the Corgi softly, "that honours don't count at duplicate."

Chapter 12

THE BIG MINOR

"You all kowtow to him so obsequiously," cried Papa indignantly, "that he has come to think he's the best player in the world. Why, it wouldn't surprise me if he thought he was better than I am!"

"Because my alleged partners allow him time and again to get away with murder," stormed the Hog, "the Greek seems to imagine he's in my class. One day I'll get a partner who can tell one suit from another. I'll mangle him. I'll. . ."

That's how it all started. Papa and the Hog had had, once again, a difference of opinion. As always, both were right and each, in turn, was resolved to prove that he was a better man than the other. How could the matter be put to the test?

Peregrine the Penguin summed up the problem in a nutshell: "We could organise a contest in which they played against each other till the cards evened out, at say, 10,000 points—more if need be. But even that wouldn't be conclusive. The loser would blame his partner, and for all we know he might be right. If only," mused the Penguin, "someone devised a bridge computer, omniscient, infallible. . ."

Oscar the Owl hooted softly, and a gleam came into his round amber eyes. "I have an idea," he said. "We can't find them players who never do wrong, but we can achieve the same result by picking them partners who never do right. So long as they were absolutely bad, so to speak, they would cancel each other out."

"One of them might slip and omit some mistake," objected P.P.

"Not if we selected the Rabbit and the Toucan," replied O.O. "The risk would be negligible."

The rest of the arrangements caused little trouble, and the

stage was soon set for the match of the year: the Hideous Hog versus Themistocles Papadopoulos.

Both sides started hot favourites. The Greek, laying 3–1 on himself, was compelled unfortunately to close his book within the hour. The Treasury, he explained, would not give him permission to take the Hog's sterling out of the country.

H.H. confided that in Zurich the gnomes were offering 5–1 against Papa. Not being commercially minded himself, and having no wish to go to Zurich, he was willing to take even money in London.

On the eve of the match there was a high-level conference at the Griffins between H.H. and R.R., who was to be his partner during the first half. Thereafter, if there was a thereafter, they would change partners.

"As you know, dear friend," began the Hideous Hog, "I have the utmost confidence in you. Of course we all have, er, little weaknesses, and I have observed that in your own case the bidding and card play are not always on the same high level as the rest of your game. On the other hand, I know no one whom I would sooner see in charge of the dummy. So I suggest," went on the Hog, "that we play the Big Minor, an ultra-modern system, ideally suited to our purpose. When you hold a notrump hand you will open 1 ♣ and I will bid notrumps. When you have a major you will open 1 ◇ and I will call your suit."

"But how will you know which one it is?" asked the Rabbit.

"No problem," the Hog assured him: "my own holding and opponents' bids will tell me all I want to know. Just leave it to me."

Papa's orders to Timothy were brief and to the point: "When in doubt, double. Fear nothing and don't forget: I am the better side and we know it."

T.T. Sees Twenty Spades

The Big Minor was severely tested in the first deal of the match:

Dealer South—Love All

H.H.
- ♠ 3
- ♡ K 7 3 2
- ◇ A K 8
- ♣ J 10 9 7 4

Papa
- ♠ 5
- ♡ Q J 10 9
- ◇ Q J 9 7
- ♣ A K 8 5

```
      N
   W     E
      S
```

T.T.
- ♠ K 10 9 8 7
- ♡ 8 4
- ◇ 10 6
- ♣ Q 6 3 2

R.R.
- ♠ A Q J 6 4 2
- ♡ A 6 5
- ◇ 5 4 3 2
- ♣ —

South	West	North	East
1 ◇	Pass	3 NT	Pass
4 ♠	Dble	Redble	

Opening Lead: ♣ K

When the Hog responded 3 NT to the conventional opening of 1◇, the Rabbit's ears dipped in perplexity. Surely 1 ♣, not 1 ◇, was the transfer bid for notrumps. Could he have made a mistake? Such things had happened to him before and oh, how cross the Hog would be if he let him down on the first deal of the match. It was taking a liberty to bid his own suit, but all in all it seemed the safest thing to do. Tremulously, with downcast eyelashes, R.R. called 4 ♠.

Sensing what had happened, Papa doubled exultantly. A double always unnerved the Rabbit, and anyway he rarely made ten tricks. With a snarl and a vicious bite at Oscar's cigar, the Hog redoubled. It might cost an extra 500, but the odds were with him. The Toucan, visibly overawed by the occasion, with kibitzers breathing down his neck, was bouncing giddily in his chair. A redouble was just the thing to stampede him into a rescue bid and a penalty of 900 or so. It was worth trying.

To the bewildered Toucan it seemed there must be at least twenty spades in the pack, but he just managed to gurgle a pass, and without further incident the Greek opened the ♣ K.

"Two down," I heard one Griffin whisper to another as the Hog tabled his hand. "The trump finesse doesn't help, so he must lose two trumps, a heart and two diamonds. Everything's wrong. Unlucky to pick up such a hand at the start of the match."

The Rabbit ruffed the ♣ K, crossed to dummy with the ♢A and ruffed a second club. After cashing the ♡ A, he went over to the table twice with the red kings to ruff two more clubs in the closed hand. That left him with ♠ A Q ♡ 6 ♢ 5 4 ♣ —. He played a diamond and, much to his surprise, the Toucan trumped his partner's queen and led a trump. With a sigh of resignation, the Rabbit put on the queen, murmuring: "One down." But it was not to be. He had made nine tricks already, and it was ruled that even R.R. would have to take one more with the ace of trumps.

"Don't think," the Rabbit assured me later, "that I would have played the hand upside down, as I did, if Papa hadn't put me off by doubling. I know all about those chaps who sell matches because they didn't draw trumps, but what's the use of finessing and all that when you know before you start that there's king to umpteen sitting over you?"

"You will observe," said Colin the Corgi as the next hand was being dealt, "that 3 NT is unmakable while 4 ♠ is unbeatable, despite the bad breaks. I am beginning to like the Big Minor."

2 + 2 = 3

Another system hand came up before long. The Hog—shown as South for the sake of convenience—picked up ♠ — ♡ 5 4 3 2 ♢ A J 5 ♣ A J 9 6 4 3.

After a pass from the Toucan, the Rabbit opened 3 ♢. At unfavourable vulnerability it couldn't be weak. Papa bid 3 ♡, and the Hog weighed up the value of his holding in a spade contract.

With 10 points and a six-card suit he felt he had enough to raise himself to game. Admittedly, a void in trumps was an embarrassment, but as against that, *he* would be playing the hand and he didn't need as many trumps as do most people.

This was the deal in full:

Dealer West— N/S Vulnerable

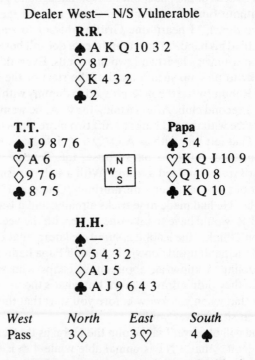

R.R.
♠ A K Q 10 3 2
♡ 8 7
♢ K 4 3 2
♣ 2

T.T.
♠ J 9 8 7 6
♡ A 6
♢ 9 7 6
♣ 8 7 5

Papa
♠ 5 4
♡ K Q J 10 9
♢ Q 10 8
♣ K Q 10

H.H.
♠ —
♡ 5 4 3 2
♢ A J 5
♣ A J 9 6 4 3

West	North	East	South
Pass	3 ♢	3 ♡	4 ♠

The Toucan opened the ♡ A and followed with the six to Papa's nine. Winning the club switch at trick three, the Hog entered dummy by ruffing a club and led out the three top spades, bringing to light the unlucky trump break.

"Having lost two hearts, he can't afford to lose two trumps as well," pointed out a kibitzer with a flair for figures.

"That's what comes of overbidding on a void," observed another sagely.

The Hideous Hog led the deuce of diamonds, finessed successfully against Papa's queen and ruffed another club on the table, leaving this four-card end position:

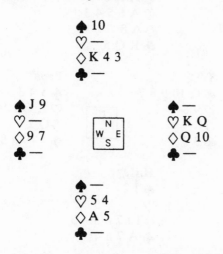

♠ 10
♡ —
◇ K 4 3
♣ —

♠ J 9   ♠ —
♡ —   ♡ K Q
◇ 9 7   ◇ Q 10
♣ —   ♣ —

♠ —
♡ 5 4
◇ A 5
♣ —

The ◇ K was followed by another to the ◇ A on the closed hand, and now a heart, through the Toucan's ♠ J 9 up to the ♠ 10 in dummy, assured the tenth decisive trick.

"What atrocious bidding!" exclaimed Papa in disgust. "A game on 22 points and a complete misfit."

"But that's just it," retorted the Hog, grinning maliciously and winking at the kibitzers. "On what other system could you reach 4 ♠ with that lot? Yet you can't break it, and there's no game elsewhere. You should learn the Big Minor, Themistocles. I am sure R.R. would be glad to give you a few lessons."

A Homicide Squeeze

Another aspect of the system claimed attention a few hands later:

R.R.
- ♠ A K 6
- ♡ A 6 5 4 3
- ◇ A 8
- ♣ K Q 5

T.T.
- ♠ Q 10 9 8 7
- ♡ 9 8 7
- ◇ K J 9
- ♣ 3 2

```
  N
W   E
  S
```

Papa
- ♠ 5 4 3
- ♡ K Q J 10
- ◇ Q 2
- ♣ J 10 9 8

H.H.
- ♠ J 2
- ♡ 2
- ◇ 10 7 6 5 4 3
- ♣ A 7 6 4

West	North	East	South
Pass	1 ◇	1 ♡	1 ♠
Pass	3 NT	Pass	Pass
Dble	Pass	Pass	4 ◇
Dble	4 ♠	Pass	Pass
Dble			

The Rabbit opened 1 ◇ conventionally, and Papa, knowing the system and getting ready to defend a spade contract, made a lead-directing overcall of 1 ♡. This the Hog could have passed with an easy conscience, but since he could bid the Rabbit's spades at the one level, it seemed too good an opportunity to miss.

In fairness to the Rabbit, it must be said that he knew from the first that his suit was hearts, not spades. But how could he convey this to the Hog, who had clearly been misled by Papa's overcall? The obvious answer was 3 NT, and R.R. might well have been allowed to play his second hand that evening had the Toucan not decided to double 3 NT for a spade lead.

Even before the double, the scales had fallen from the Hog's eyes. He knew that the Rabbit wouldn't dare to bid notrumps except in a dire emergency. But if hearts were his suit, he might have no guard in spades, and if so, 3 NT could prove expensive: hence the rescue into 4 ◇. With a deep sigh, the Rabbit gave preference.

Having started to double, the Toucan did not like to leave off, and for once H.H. refrained from redoubling.

Winning the heart lead with the ace, the Hog ruffed a heart in the closed hand and, going over to the table with the ♣ Q, ruffed another heart. Crossing to dummy with the ♣ K, he led out the ace and king of trumps and continued with the six, throwing diamonds from his hand. Then he sat back to await developments.

The Toucan won the third trump trick and played the ♠ Q, just in case there were any lurkers. The Hog discarded a heart from dummy and another diamond from his hand, while Papa parted with the deuce of diamonds. These were the last four cards:

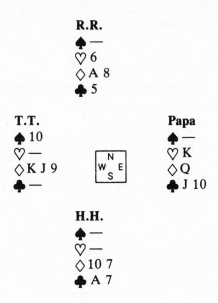

```
                    R.R.
                    ♠ —
                    ♡ 6
                    ◇ A 8
                    ♣ 5

    T.T.                            Papa
    ♠ 10            ┌─────┐         ♠ —
    ♡ —            │  N  │         ♡ K
    ◇ K J 9        │W   E│         ◇ Q
    ♣ —            │  S  │         ♣ J 10
                    └─────┘
                    H.H.
                    ♠ —
                    ♡ —
                    ◇ 10 7
                    ♣ A 7
```

Reluctant to lead away from his ◇ K, especially after seeing Papa's deuce, the Toucan played his last spade. The ◇8, the ◇Q and the ◇ 7 completed the trick. Now the Toucan had only diamonds left, but he didn't mind leading one, for dummy's ace was bare. Why, he wondered, was Papa wincing and gnashing his teeth?

"A suicide squeeze," said Oscar the Owl.

"A homicide squeeze, you mean," cried the Greek bitterly. "Why did you play that last spade, Timothy? What have I ever done to you?"

"Why did you deceive me by dropping the ◇2?" countered the Toucan.

"Please note," observed Colin the Corgi, "that though 4 ♠ isn't exactly foolproof, the only other game contract. . ."

"Eleven top tricks in 5 ◇," interjected someone.

"Quite wrong," replied the Hog. "We are not concerned with top tricks, but only with the ones we could make, and in 5 ◇ the lead would run up to the wrong hand. When R.R. is declarer," added H.H. by way of explanation, "the lead always runs up to the wrong hand. It's one of the facts of life."

Dummy Reversal

An unsuspected flaw in the Big Minor caused a systemic hitch in the next rubber.

Dealer South—Love All

H.H.
♠ —
♡ K 2
◇ A K Q J 10 9 3 2
♣ K 3 2

Papa
♠ A K 4 3 2
♡ A Q J
◇ 7
♣ A 10 9 4

| |
| N |
| W   E |
| S |

T.T.
♠ J
♡ 10 9 8 7 6 5 4
◇ 8
♣ 8 7 6 5

R.R.
♠ Q 10 9 8 7 6 5
♡ 3
◇ 6 5 4
♣ Q J

South	West	North	East
3 ◇	Pass	3 NT	Pass
Pass	Dble	Pass	4 ♡
Pass	Pass	5 ◇	Pass
Pass	5 ♡	Pass	Pass
6 ◇	Dble	Redble	6 ♡
7 ◇	Dble		

The system made no provision for the type of hand on which declarer—that is, the Hog—would have length and strength in the suit bid conventionally by dummy-presumptive.

The auction started in orderly fashion, but when the Toucan decided to take out Papa's double of 3 NT into 4 ♡, the Hog was driven into what he later described as a dummy reversal.

Deeply flattered that he should be allowed to play a hand, the Rabbit had no hesitation in bidding 6 ◇ over 5 ♡.

"I had nothing, of course, which is exactly what I promised," he explained later. "But I had nothing in the right places, if you see what I mean."

The Greek doubled exultantly. Not for one moment did the Hog expect to make 6 ◇. Hence the redouble, vicious and snarling, calculated to intimidate players of tougher fibre than the Toucan.

The stage was set for a clash of willpower. The Hog willed the Toucan to bid. Papa willed him to pass. Giddily, the Toucan bounced up and down. Finally subsiding, he burbled in a weak, hesitant voice: "6 ♡."

The Hog's features broke into a triumphant smile. Papa, beaten, sank in his chair. But victor and vanquished alike had reckoned without the Rabbit. Oblivious to the hot waves of hatred emanating from his partner, R.R. called 7 ◇.

As he doubled, the Greek, with a pitying look offered H.H. a black, gold-tipped cigarette, watching him wince at the sight of the monogram.

Papa led the ♠ K.

Tabling his hand, the Hog, always thoughtful, spread out the diamonds with the Q J 10 protruding invitingly in a small bulge. Picking the nearest card, R.R. ruffed with the ◇J, cashed the ◇Q and sat back, as was his wont after the first few tricks, to study the hand.

When a recount confirmed that there were no more diamonds out, it suddenly dawned on him that he had two trump entries in the closed hand, and remembering the Toucan's jack at trick one, he decided to set up the spades. He was made to play the hand to the bitter end, but there was no defence.

"You showed excellent judgment in not redoubling," said the Hog approvingly. "They might have found a cheap save in 7 ♡." Then, turning to the kibitzers, he added: "Mr Papadopoulos has been playing a lot of duplicate lately, and these light doubles often pay in pairs events."

"Well played," said the Toucan admiringly.

"I needed a 1–1 trump break," explained the Rabbit, "but when all's said and done, it's no worse than an even-money chance, is it?"

Chapter 13

S.B. STRIKES AGAIN

As we waited for the lobster soufflé, the Hog munched olives in gloomy silence.

He was in a bad mood. He had dieted since teatime, and he was still wincing with pain from the wounds inflicted on him by the Rabbit, the Walrus and the Secretary Bird, especially the latter. Their ministrations had been hard to endure, too hard on an empty stomach.

My sympathy went out to H.H., for I had watched that last rubber before dinner, in which he had had to suffer so much. This is how it started:

Dealer South—Love All

W.W.
♠ A 5 4
♡ A Q 8
◇ A 9 8
♣ 6 5 4 3

S.B.
♠ 10 9 8 7 6
♡ 7 6 5
◇ K Q J 10
♣ A

H.H.
♠ K 3 2
♡ J 10 9
◇ 7 6 5
♣ 10 9 8 7

R.R.
♠ Q J
♡ K 4 3 2
◇ 4 3 2
♣ K Q J 2

South	West	North	East
Pass	Pass	1 ♣	Pass
2 NT	Pass	3 NT	

The bidding was quite straightforward. With fourteen points the Walrus was too strong to open 1 NT, which he would have called on a mere thirteen and a half. The Rabbit was happy to play the hand, for while he was prepared to admit that he might be the second-worst player in the universe, he felt certain that even he could not wrest the world title from Walter the Walrus.

The Emeritus Professor of Bio-Sophistry opened the ◇K. The Rueful Rabbit held up his ace till the end, and sighed with relief when the Hideous Hog followed suit on the third round. At the fourth trick the Rabbit led a club from dummy to the king and ace. The Secretary Bird cashed his long diamond, and H.H. was in trouble. If he parted with the ♠ 3, it would discourage the spade switch he wanted. If he threw the ♡ 9, it would look as if he wanted hearts. Either way, he would convey the misleading impression that he preferred the red major to the black.

R.R., throwing the deuce of clubs from his hand, discarded one of dummy's spades and, with a growl, the Hog too let go a baby spade. As he had feared, the Secretary Bird continued with the ♡ 7 and the Rabbit, winning in dummy, played two more rounds, watching anxiously to see if the suit would break. When all followed to the king he smiled happily, for he could see nine tricks: a spade, four hearts, a diamond and three clubs.

"I hope I haven't given you too much to do," said the Walrus; "but we should have the requisite 25–26."

"You were perfectly right," dithered the Rabbit joyfully. "I mean, all's well now. We're home. Everything's cut and dried. That is. . .mm. . .mm. . ."

There was a dangerous gleam behind the Emeritus Professor's glasses and the white tufts of bristly hair, projecting at right angles from behind his ears, stiffened visibly. Uncrossing his long, wiry legs and throwing a spade on the queen of clubs—which R.R. played before his last heart—he enquired in sibilant tones:

"Are you making a claim?"

"No, no, of course not," replied the Rabbit, startled to see S.B. show out in clubs. "It was just that I could see nine tricks. . .I mean if. . .that is, when. . ."

"Will you be good enough to expose your cards and indicate how you propose to play them?" hissed S.B.

"I. . .we. . ." spluttered the Rabbit. "I was not going to draw trumps or. . .er. . ."

"A handsome concession in a notrump contract," conceded the Professor, "but you are aware, of course, that you may not finesse unless you. . ."

"Nonsense," cried the outraged Hog, looking lovingly at his ♠ K. "He can finesse if. . ."

"He can do no such thing," broke in S.B. in acid tones, his Adam's apple throbbing with hatred of the Hog. "He should have stated specifically. . ."

"Stop, please stop. The question does not arise," interrupted the Rueful Rabbit in a tremulous voice. With shaking fingers he played his last heart, throwing a spade demonstratively from dummy, so that no finesse should be possible any longer. This was the position:

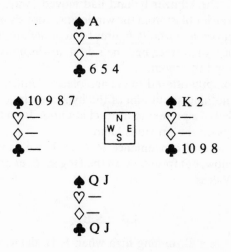

```
                    ♠ A
                    ♡ —
                    ◇ —
                    ♣ 6 5 4

    ♠ 10 9 8 7              ♠ K 2
    ♡ —          N         ♡ —
    ◇ —        W   E       ◇ —
    ♣ —          S         ♣ 10 9 8

                    ♠ Q J
                    ♡ —
                    ◇ —
                    ♣ Q J
```

"Sorry, Walter," he said meekly. "Had I not spoken hastily —not that I meant anything, mind you—I could still take the spade finesse, but I much prefer to go down than to have all this, er, bad feeling. It's most upsetting. Most."

The Hog gnashed his teeth in fury and frustration. If he threw a club, dummy's last club would be good. If he bared the ♠ K, R.R. could make his ninth trick with the ♠ Q with which he was marked on the bidding. The Professor's purblind insistence on the letter of the law had driven the Rueful Rabbit into executing unconsciously a Criss-Cross squeeze—something of which he had never heard.

"That H.H., of all people, should let me make that ♠ Q!" was his only comment when the hand was over.

"I hope you are proud of all your quibbling," said the Hog bitterly to his partner.

"Why did you discard the ♠ 3, inviting a heart switch?" counterattacked S.B. "But for that, we should have broken the contract."

"In future," rejoined the Hog scathingly, "leave *me* to invoke the laws. At least I know whose side I am on."

The Walrus was too occupied with bigger things to follow these exchanges. The kibitzer behind had moved away, leaving him exposed to an icy blast from the window. Anxiously he thought of the rising curve in mortality figures from bronchitis, pleurisy and pneumonia. "I am freezing," he said in a whisper which reverberated round the room.

R.R. promptly offered to change places. Unlike the Walrus, there was nothing about him of the hypochondriac, and he was only too glad of a pretext to distract attention from the unhappy contretemps on the previous hand.

For the sake of convenience R.R. is shown as South in the diagram below, but from now on the Hog sat over him, with S.B. over the Walrus.

S.B. *v* S.B.

Feelings were still running high when H.H. dealt, and through force of habit opened 1 ♡, that being the lead he was most anxious to discourage in the predestined contract of 3 NT:

Dealer West—Game All

W.W.
♠ K 8 7
♡ 7 6
◇ 9 8 7 6
♣ 9 8 7 6

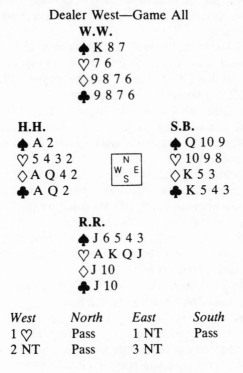

H.H.
♠ A 2
♡ 5 4 3 2
◇ A Q 4 2
♣ A Q 2

S.B.
♠ Q 10 9
♡ 10 9 8
◇ K 5 3
♣ K 5 4 3

R.R.
♠ J 6 5 4 3
♡ A K Q J
◇ J 10
♣ J 10

West	North	East	South
1 ♡	Pass	1 NT	Pass
2 NT	Pass	3 NT	

The Walrus passed and the Emeritus Professor called 1 NT, thereby staking his claim to play the hand.

Still tense and flustered, the Rueful Rabbit was sorting his hand with quivering fingers. Almost every card was in place, the red suits alternating neatly with the black, when the ♡ A suddenly slipped on the table.

"Oh dear, oh dear," exclaimed the Rabbit blushing guiltily.

"Card exposed during the auction," snapped S.B. His glasses flashed triumphantly with a telepathic message to the Hog: "You can't keep a good man down," he seemed to say, "and I'll invoke the laws as much as I please. So there!"

The Secretary Bird barred a heart lead, and after trying most of his cards in turn, some of them twice, R.R. settled finally on the ◇J. A spade might have saved time, perhaps, but the opening made little difference. Declarer had seven tricks on top and he made no more.

"Thank goodness," said R.R., sighing with relief. "But for my lapse, I would have taken the first four tricks, anyway, of course, I am so glad that I did not give away the contract. Please forgive me. It's all this tension. . .so unnecessary."

S.B. shrugged his narrow, sloping shoulders. "Nothing to the hand," he remarked casually. "I could not make the contract anyway, for no suit broke and once I surrendered the lead they would come in with four hearts."

"I congratulate you," bellowed the Hideous Hog. "You are the only man I know who has succeeded in committing suicide twice in ten minutes—and with the same weapon, too!"

"Are you suggesting. . ." began S.B.

"Yes, I am," roared H.H. "Had you allowed R.R. to lead out his hearts peacefully, as he was about to do, even you could not have avoided making 3 NT."

"I have only seven tricks—eight, if I play for one down and guess the spade position," persisted S.B.

"Ridiculous!" expostulated W.W. indignantly. "I only had three points. Try squeezing me out of that. Ha!"

"And what do you discard on the fourth heart?" went on the Hog. "Whatever card you play, it will cost you two tricks."

On the third heart W.W. could have thrown a spade, but his next discard was bound to present declarer with a trick in clubs or diamonds or with the ♠ Q. Then, on declarer's eighth winner, W.W. would have been squeezed again in the other two suits. There was no escape from a progressive squeeze—so long as R.R. took the first four tricks.

"There's not a breath of air in the room," complained the Walrus. "It's stifling."

He dealt and was allowed to play the hand in 1 ◇, "One down," said the Hog. It sounded like '1 ◇', and R.R. duly inscribed 20 below the line.

R.R. Bids to the Score

The Walrus dealt with the wrong pack, but nobody noticed. The Hideous Hog and the Secretary Bird were too busy generating ill feeling towards each other. The Rueful Rabbit was trying to remember his telephone number, which had recently been changed, while the Walrus himself was thinking anxiously of all the germs which were whirling round him as he dealt:

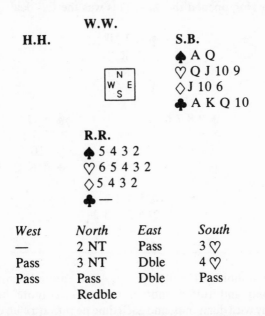

W.W.

H.H.

S.B.
♠ A Q
♡ Q J 10 9
◇ J 10 6
♣ A K Q 10

R.R.
♠ 5 4 3 2
♡ 6 5 4 3 2
◇ 5 4 3 2
♣ —

West	North	East	South
—	2 NT	Pass	3 ♡
Pass	3 NT	Dble	4 ♡
Pass	Pass	Dble	Pass
	Redble		

I was sitting between the Rabbit and the Secretary Bird when the Walrus opened, unexpectedly, 2 NT. S.B. passed with a cunning look, while R.R. fidgeted uncomfortably in his chair. He glanced at the score, shook his head and wrinkled his long, sensitive nose. Then he looked at his scorepad again and bid 3 ♡. After all, it was only one more and they needed it for game—or so he thought.

The Hog passed and the Walrus began to call 3 NT. Half-way through, the Emeritus Professor of Bio-Sophistry broke the sound barrier with a pulverising double which shook the Rabbit from head to foot. With downcast eyes he mumbled "4 ♡." He expected, of course, to go down a packet, but a smaller packet in hearts than in notrumps.

The Walrus reckoned that he had almost an entire point to spare, and though it went against the grain to redouble when the Rabbit was at the wheel, he, too, had been caught up in the feverish atmosphere round the table.

The Hog opened the ♣ 9. This was the full deal:

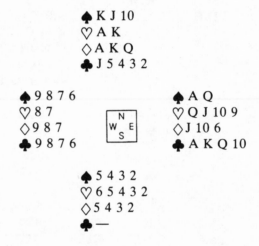

```
              ♠ K J 10
              ♡ A K
              ◇ A K Q
              ♣ J 5 4 3 2

   ♠ 9 8 7 6                    ♠ A Q
   ♡ 8 7           N            ♡ Q J 10 9
   ◇ 9 8 7      W     E         ◇ J 10 6
   ♣ 9 8 7 6       S            ♣ A K Q 10

              ♠ 5 4 3 2
              ♡ 6 5 4 3 2
              ◇ 5 4 3 2
              ♣ —
```

The Rabbit ruffed the opening lead, entered dummy with a diamond and ruffed another club. Twice more he entered dummy with diamonds, and each time he ruffed a club on the way back. This was the six-card end position:

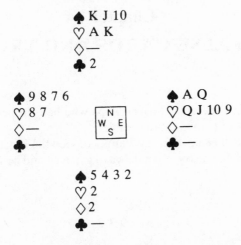

♠ K J 10
♡ A K
◇ —
♣ 2

♠ 9 8 7 6   ♠ A Q
♡ 8 7   ♡ Q J 10 9
◇ —   ◇ —
♣ —   ♣ —

♠ 5 4 3 2
♡ 2
◇ 2
♣ —

Now the Rabbit played a trump and cashed dummy's ace and king, removing the Hog's two trumps. Having collected nine tricks, he sat back happily, for he had never hoped to get out of it so cheaply. Nonchalantly he led dummy's ♣ 2, not caring much whether it was good or not. He knew well enough that several trumps were out against him, and S.B. was clearly marked with the ♠ A Q.

The Professor was, however, powerless. Whatever the order in which he played his cards, he was obliged to lead spades into dummy's tenace.

"Half a dummy reversal and half an endplay," observed Oscar the Owl.

"Surprising what one can do if only one is sufficiently frightened," remarked Peregrine the Penguin.

"Doubling on tram tickets," growled the Hideous Hog.

"Only lead. . ." began the Secretary Bird, when the Walrus who had been working something out, broke in, shaking a fat forefinger at the Rueful Rabbit.

"How many points did you have?" he asked in menacing tones.

Chapter 14

FALSE CARDS AND TRUE

"Anyone vulnerable?" asked Papa who had strolled over after being cut out from another table.

"We shall be up after this hand," replied the Emeritus Professor of Bio-Sophistry. His side was a game up and he was declarer in 4 ♠:

R.R.
♠ J 9 3 2
♡ 7 4
◇ 9 7 6 5
♣ A Q 10

W.W.

```
  N
W   E
  S
```

H.H.

S.B.
♠ K Q 10 7 6 4
♡ A K 3
◇ 2
♣ 9 6 4

South	North
1 ♠	2 ♠
3 ♠	4 ♠

The final contract was due to a routine misunderstanding. The Professor, better known as the Secretary Bird, had raised the spades to the three level pre-emptively, to shut out hearts. The Rabbit, busy with a muffin, had no time for such refinements and bid game automatically. Part-score contracts were so dull.

Walter the Walrus opened the ◇ K and continued with the queen. S.B. ruffed, led a spade to Walter's ace, ruffed the diamond return and drew the last enemy trump. It was at this point that the Greek had enquired about the state of the rubber.

"I can, in fact, put my hand down," S.B. assured him, "for all that's left is a baby elimination. However, it usually saves time to play them out. Not all of us," he added with a meaning wink in the direction of the Walrus, "are as quick on the uptake as we might be."

"What do you make the difference?" asked the Hideous Hog, turning to the Rabbit, one of whose New Year resolutions was to keep a running total of the score with every hand. "Is that 230 I see?"

The Rabbit nodded gravely. The large, bold figures on his pad were unmistakable. There was 30 above the line, 60 and 150 below. The total inscribed at the top of the 'We' column read 230.

The Rabbit was proud of his new method of scoring, which showed at a glance when an extra trick would affect the rubber points.

Swinging his long sinewy arms rhythmically, not unlike a metronome, the Secretary Bird cashed his two top hearts and ruffed the third in dummy. Then he trumped the table's last diamond in his hand and led a club. The red suits having been eliminated, dummy was left with the deuce of spades and the A Q 10 of clubs. Declarer's last four cards were three small clubs and the king of spades.

"As you can see," said the Professor, "even if the club finesse fails, I am home, for H.H. will have to lead another club into dummy's A 10 or concede a ruff and discard." The ♣ Q, however, held the trick, the Hog following with the jack. S.B. looked up.

"Did you say that we were 230 up?" he asked with sudden interest. R.R. agreed. Returning to his hand with the last trump, S.B. led a club, finessing dummy's ten. The Hog promptly won with the king and scored the last trick with the ♡ Q. One down. This was the complete deal:

R.R.
♠ J 9 3 2
♡ 7 4
◇ 9 7 6 5
♣ A Q 10

W.W.
♠ A
♡ J 10 6
◇ K Q J 4
♣ 8 7 5 3 2

```
  N
W   E
  S
```

H.H.
♠ 8 5
♡ Q 9 8 5 2
◇ A 10 8 3
♣ K J

S.B.
♠ K Q 10 7 6 4
♡ A K 3
◇ 2
♣ 9 6 4

"Very cunning, H.H.," observed Oscar the Owl. "At the risk of a hundred points you defeated an unbeatable game."

"You are too kind," gloated the Hog happily; "but I wasn't really risking anything, you know. I didn't like to contradict our friend, but I think he has made a slight error. The difference in the scores is 240, not 230—or rather it *was* 240. Now, of course, it is 140. Ha! ha! Anyway," continued H.H., "eleven tricks came to no more than ten, if you see what I mean, ha! ha! ha!"

Themistocles Papadopoulos looked pityingly at us all. "Taking candy from children! You'd think that none of you had seen a false card before," he said, adding contemptuously: "I should like him to try that trick on me some day."

Bath Coup—Hog Variation

The rubber was soon over. Muttering dark imprecations and hissing in accompaniment, the Secretary Bird cut out and the Greek took his place. Before long he was defending a contract of 5 ◇:

R.R.
♠ 7 6 2
♡ 2
◇ 10 7 6
♣ Q J 10 9 8 7

Papa　　　　　　　　　**W.W.**
♠ J 5 4
♡ K Q 5 4
◇ A 5 4
♣ 6 3 2

```
    N
  W   E
    S
```

H.H.

South	North
2 ◇	3 ◇
3 NT	4 ♣
5 ◇	

The Greek opened the ♡ K and noted with suspicion that as the Rueful Rabbit tabled his hand, the Hog said nothing. Not an oath, not an insult. Why not? Surely his bidding called for a few well chosen words of vilification. Papa shook his head uneasily.

The ♡ K brought the six from the Walrus and the three from the Hog. With one trick in the bag and the ace of trumps to come, the Greek looked anxiously for one more trick to beat the contract. Miracles apart, spades alone offered any real hope, so at trick two, Papa switched to the ♠ 4, bringing the queen from his partner and the ace from declarer. The ◇K came next. All followed and Papa held off. The Hog continued with the ♣ A and ♣ K—the Walrus contributing the five and the four—and then reverted to trumps. Papa couldn't afford to play low a second time, for if he did, H.H. would ruff a heart in dummy and throw two losers on the clubs. Papa, of course, would ruff the fourth club with his ace, but it would be too late.

The Greek took stock. Since the Hog had shown up with no more than five trumps and no ♡ A, he badly needed the ♠ K to make up the values for his opening two-bid. Papa's only hope of beating the contract was surely to kill dummy's entry to the clubs while he still had a small trump. That way the Hog would be kept to ten tricks—four trumps, the ace and king of spades, a heart ruff and three clubs. Having checked and cross-checked his calculations, the Greek led a low heart to knock out dummy's trump entry. Instead of ruffing, however, the Hog ran the heart up to his jack, and drawing the last trump, claimed the rest of the tricks. These were the four hands:

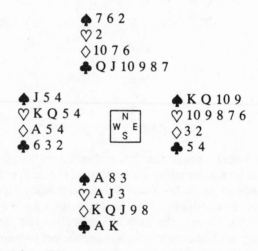

♠ 7 6 2
♥ 2
♦ 10 7 6
♣ Q J 10 9 8 7

♠ J 5 4
♥ K Q 5 4
♦ A 5 4
♣ 6 3 2

♠ K Q 10 9
♥ 10 9 8 7 6
♦ 3 2
♣ 5 4

♠ A 8 3
♥ A J 3
♦ K Q J 9 8
♣ A K

"That, my dear Papa, should teach you a lesson," said the Hideous Hog severely. "People who fall for Bath Coups shouldn't jeer at others." The Hog nudged Oscar in the ribs to make sure that he did not miss that quip about the Bath Coup. Papa's Adam's apple shot out three millimetres and there was a deep growl at the back of his throat, but nothing concrete materialised. Silently he vowed vengeance.

H.H. is Taken In

The gods on Mount Olympus must have heard him, for a chance to turn the tables on his enemy came within the hour. I heard about it from Colin the Corgi, who was showing this hand around over the preprandial Madeira at the Griffins bar:

Dealer South—Love All

♠ 4 3
♡ 10 4
◇ A K 4
♣ Q J 10 9 6 4

```
      N
   W     E
      S
```

♠ A 5 2
♡ A 9 7 6
◇ 9 7 3
♣ A 8 7

South	North
1 NT	3 NT

"West leads the ♠ 7 and East plays the jack. Your move, Oscar."

"Where's Papa and where's the Hog," asked the Owl, "and who are their respective partners?"

"You'll savour the hand better if I keep you in suspense for a bit," replied C.C. "Meanwhile, it's your turn to play."

"The ♠ 5," vouchsafed O.O. after a cursory glance at the hand.

"Yes," echoed the Rabbit, "to rectify the count for a squeeze."

The Corgi didn't give him so much as a withering look. "Aren't you missing something?" he asked Oscar. "Since the vital club finesse must be taken into the West hand, a hold-up can surely serve no purpose."

"And how can it help to go up with the ace?" countered O.O.

"Because there's scope here for a pretty piece of deception," replied C.C. "Give some thought to that spade suit. East's jack at trick one denies the ten. So West has it. And, of course, if East had the king he would have played it. So West has the king, too. Now from a suit headed by the K Q 10 he would have surely led the king, not the seven. It follows that West has the K 10 and East the queen, though West can't be certain of it.

"Seeing declarer grab the first trick with the ace, a cultured West may be suspicious. After all, isn't it a classical piece of deception to win the first trick with the ace, holding A Q, when another suit is wide open? Here it might well be hearts."

The Rabbit's ears twitched nervously. "No, no, he's not rectifying anything," C.C. assured him. "The idea is to deter West from switching. If he controls the long suit, as would be the case here if he had the ♣ K, he is intended to lead another spade, fondly imagining that his partner has the queen. Of course, both the Hog and Papa are thoroughly familiar with this stratagem."

"In fact," explained Oscar to the Rabbit, who wasn't quite with it, "going up with the ace can be a trap to make West suspect a trap that isn't there."

"And did West fall into the trap?" asked R.R.

Filling in the hands, the Corgi unfolded the rest of the story:

Declarer won the first trick with the ♠ A and, crossing to the ◇ K, took the club finesse. West played low nonchalantly, allowing the queen to hold. The ♣ J came next. East, who had followed with the ♣ 3 to the first trick, now played the deuce. Declarer ran the jack and, well, you can guess the rest. West grabbed the trick with his lone king and promptly returned the ♢ Q, killing the entry to the clubs, now blocked by the ace in the closed hand.

"Very pretty," said O.O. admiringly.

As H.H., wreathed in smiles, walked into the bar, the Corgi told us: "Papa was thé luckless declarer with Walter the Walrus as his partner. H.H was playing with me."

"That poor Papa!" chortled the Hog. "The funny part is that he took me in completely with that ♠ A. He banged it down so confidently that I felt sure he had the queen behind it. Just what he would do, too, if he were worried about the hearts. You should have seen his expression when I produced the ♢Q simultaneously with the ♣ K. Ha! ha!"

Oscar frowned. "It was a good and a daring defence, but is that any reason to sneer at Papa?" he asked reprovingly. "Had the roles been reversed, Papa might well have held up the ♣ K, just as you did, and you would have doubtless fallen for it in the same way."

"Never." The Hog shook his head vigorously. "Didn't Colin tell you how the Walrus followed to the clubs, first the three, then the two? Would he do such a thing unless he had a doubleton? Perish the thought. Just as he counts points, regardless of the consequences, so he signals as a moral duty. It's the decent thing to do. Our Walter, as we all know, has the highest principles and the lowest I.Q. in the club. Well, the co-lowest, anyway," added H.H., correcting himself as the Rabbit and the Toucan walked in. "And there was Papa, always so busy being clever that he has no time to notice how stupid other people can be. Such an egocentric! No wonder he so often outwits himself."

Chapter 15

HANDICAP PROJECT

All the desks in the writing room were occupied. Members of the Griffins Club were writing their letters of resignation. Softly I closed the door, hoping that no .one would see me, for my conscience was far from clear. When it was mooted that we should introduce handicaps to give the weaker players a fair chance against their betters, I was the first to come out in support.

For years many of us had felt that lesser mortals should not be condemned forever to keep the Hog in champagne or Papa the Greek in Havanas, just because they were so much better than the rest of us at counting up to 13. In motor races the entries are categorised strictly according to class. Boxers fight only within their weight. Golfers have carefully adjusted handicaps. Why shouldn't the same principle apply to bridge?

Alas, little did we dream how low the pursuit of justice would lay us. The resentment of the heartless tycoons was only to be expected. What we did not foresee was the bitterness of their victims.

"It's an outrage, sir!" bellowed the Hideous Hog when he heard that I was backing the handicap. "As you know, I don't care about money. By all means, tax an art for which even the ghouls at the Treasury have so far shown some scant respect. But don't forget that in robbing me you are penalising merit, imposing a brutal levy on quality, killing enterprise. . ."

Themistocles Papadopoulos buttonholed me in the street. "The money," he explained, "is purely incidental, but there are principles at stake. You are subsidising ineptitude, rewarding failure. The worse they play, the bigger your grant to them. It's immoral. It's antisocial, it's. . ."

We could steel our hearts against the strong. But how could we face the anguished reproaches of the weak?

"I do not claim to be an expert," candidly admitted Walter the Walrus, heaving his huge bulk in front of me to cut off my escape to the cloakroom, "but surely you will not bracket me with that ridiculous Toucan? Let me tell you what he did to me only yesterday. . . ."

"Don't let me disturb you," began Timothy the Toucan when I picked up the phone at two o'clock in the morning, "but there's a rumour afoot that I'm to have the same handicap as that pathetic Walrus. I'll give you only one hand. . . ."

The meek and the humble despised each other too much to take shelter under the same umbrella. They much preferred to get wet.

Meanwhile, behind closed doors, the Handicap Advisory Committee—H.A.C., as it came to be known—was wrestling with wellnigh insoluble problems. By what standard does one measure demerit? How, for instance, should one compare the badness of Walter the Walrus with that of Timothy the Toucan?

To Walter bridge was a game of points, and he preferred to go down virtuously with the required quota than to bring home a shady contract on an overdraft. The Toucan's main difficulty was to get a count of the hand—his own. He didn't bother about the others.

Current form was a factor we had promised to take into account, and we had before us this example of Walter's prowess:

```
          ♠ 10 5
          ♡ K 7 3
          ◇ Q J 10
          ♣ A Q 10 9 4

C.C.
♠ K J 2
♡ A 2          N
◇ 6 5 4 2    W   E
♣ J 8 5 3       S
```

South	North
1 ♠	2 ♣
4 ♠	Pass

The sorrowful tale was unfolded by Colin the Corgi. Being a member of the Committee, he declared his interest, as they say in Parliament, for he was himself West and Walter was his partner.

"With two pretty certain trump tricks," began C.C., "I opened the heart ace. Walter produced the ten and declarer the four. Go on from there, Oscar," said Colin, turning to Oscar the Owl, our Senior Kibitzer. "I don't want to influence you. Just call the cards."

"The deuce of hearts, I suppose," obliged O.O., blinking his amber eyes. "No reason to switch."

"Dummy's king goes up, partner and declarer contributing the six and five respectively. Next comes the diamond ten from the board, the three from the Walrus and the ace from declarer."

"The deuce," called O.O.

"The spade ace," continued Colin.

"The deuce," again echoed Oscar.

Colin winced. "No, no, you can't mean that, Oscar. Throw your jack quickly or you will be endplayed the trick after next. Surely you must see that declarer has no losing diamond. He would have taken the finesse had he needed it. And for some reason he didn't take the trump finesse, either. Why not?"

"Maybe my partner has the bare queen," answered O.O., without much conviction.

"Very well," persisted C.C. "You follow to the spade ace with the deuce, and partner drops the singleton queen. Declarer lays down the diamond king and leads a trump. Of course, you make two trump tricks, but declarer makes five trumps, one heart, three diamonds and a club. No good, you see. To beat the contract I had to foresee the endplay and give up a trick in trumps so as to gain two in hearts."

This was the deal in full:

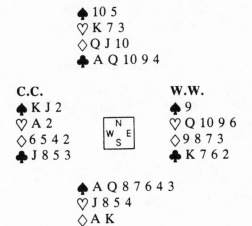

♠ 10 5
♡ K 7 3
◇ Q J 10
♣ A Q 10 9 4

C.C.
♠ K J 2
♡ A 2
◇ 6 5 4 2
♣ J 8 5 3

W.W.
♠ 9
♡ Q 10 9 6
◇ 9 8 7 3
♣ K 7 6 2

♠ A Q 8 7 6 4 3
♡ J 8 5 4
◇ A K
♣ —

"Observe that declarer wasn't especially interested in taking the spade finesse. If West had K x x, it wouldn't have helped and if he had K x, he would have been endplayed, anyway, just as I should have been had I failed to get out of the way with the jack."

"Very clever, I'm sure," said Oscar the Owl, a little testily, "but what has it to do with Walter's handicap? Did he revoke or something?"

"Worse than that," replied Colin. "He threw a heart away on the trumps, and he was so convincing in the post-mortem that the kibitzers gave him right! First he argued that in the three-card endplay he was squeezed in hearts and clubs. Declarer, he explained, must have a club, since otherwise he would have cashed the ace when he was in dummy with the heart king and still had the chance. Next he blamed me for opening the ace of hearts. Then he demanded to know how many tricks he was expected to win on his miserable five points. Finally, he rounded on me. I had given away a trick in trumps, quite blatantly, trying to be clever, so what if he, too, had lost a trick somewhere? Was there one law for members of the Committee and another for the *hoi polloi*?"

Oscar nodded sympathetically. It was galling to have a pretty defence butchered by an ignoramus. On current form W.W. seemed to deserve the maximum handicap.

Cold-Blooded Murder

I had to demur. "Not quite the maximum," I pleaded, "for at least Walter's crime was unpremeditated. Compare it with this cold-blooded murder:"

♠ A Q J 7
♡ J 7 6
◇ A K 10
♣ A K 10

♠ 9
♡ A K Q 10 9 8
◇ J 7 6
♣ J 7 6

South	West	North	East
H.H.	**T.T.**		**Papa**
—	—	2 NT	Pass
4 ♣	Pass	4 NT	Pass
7 ♡	Pass	Pass	Pass

"Fancy having to kibitz such bidding," said Colin the Corgi in disgust. "Who was South?"

"None other than the Hog," I told them. "He checked on the ace position via Gerber, but opposite a 2 NT opening his 16 points. . ."

"What 16 points?" asked O.O. and C.C. in unison.

"Why, 11 in top cards, 2 for the long hearts and 3 for his superb dummy play. That's his advanced method of hand valuation, and it usually works. Be that as it may," I added, "how do you play the hand to give yourself the best chance? A trump is opened."

"The spade finesse must be right for a start. . ." began C.C.

". . .and one of the queens might drop," ventured O.O.

"Nothing drops," I replied; "but I had better tell you how the Hog played it. He cashed dummy's two ace-kings and led out all his trumps. The spade finesse was not enough by itself, but if West also had one of the queens he would be squeezed."

Oscar the Owl blinked sagely, just as if he could see it all.

"And did West have the spade king and one of those missing queens?" asked Colin.

"Neither," I told them. "Papa, who was East, had all three. He grasped the Hog's plan at once, as soon as dummy's minor suit winners were cashed. Foreseeing the progressive squeeze, he played quickly and smoothly, like a man without a care in the world. He bared his spade king five tricks from the end, but his last three cards, of course, were the king and the two queens. These were the four hands:

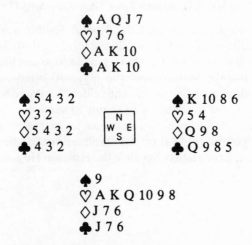

♠ A Q J 7
♥ J 7 6
♦ A K 10
♣ A K 10

♠ 5 4 3 2   ♠ K 10 8 6
♥ 3 2   ♥ 5 4
♦ 5 4 3 2 N ♦ Q 9 8
♣ 4 3 2 W E ♣ Q 9 8 5
    S

♠ 9
♥ A K Q 10 9 8
♦ J 7 6
♣ J 7 6

"Dummy," I went on, "retained the spade A Q J, while the Hog's last three cards were the spade nine and the minor suit jacks. He was now all set to take the spade finesse and destined to go three down. But this is where T.T. comes in."

Timothy was sitting West.

"What on earth could that Toucan have done?" asked the Owl, looking mystified.

"The Toucan," I explained, "felt that he had a part to play, and he decided to help Papa in his discards by giving him a count on the hand. So he carefully threw away every one of his four spades. When the Hog came to lead his spade nine, Timothy showed out and, of course, it was all over. The Greek could only gnash his teeth, but the Toucan was very upset. 'Why did Papa have to bare his king?' he asked with an injured air. 'I was so careful to throw away my spades—every one of them. Didn't he count?' "

We agreed that T.T. was entitled to a more favourable handicap than W.W. But should it be the maximum? If so, what of the Rueful Rabbit?

What Handicap for a Guardian Angel?

It was not in dispute that the Rueful Rabbit was the most hopeless, helpless, and above all, the most scatterbrained of the Griffins. But when the Committee came to assess his handicap, we had to take into account the repeated intervention of an unscrupulous guardian angel, who seldom hesitated to crown his protegé's worst misdeeds with shameful success.

This was the first exhibit which came to our notice. The Rabbit was harnessed to Walter the Walrus, the dedicated point counter, and they had cut against the Hideous Hog and Papa the Greek.

W.W.
♠ A 6 5 4
♡ 2
◇ Q 10 5 4
♣ Q 5 3 2

H.H.
♠ 9 8 7
♡ 7 6 5 4 3
◇ K 6
♣ A 10 4

	N	
W		E
	S	

Papa
♠ Q J 10
♡ —
◇ A J 9 8 2
♣ K 9 8 7 6

R.R.
♠ K 3 2
♡ A K Q J 10 9 8
◇ 7 3
♣ J

West	North	East	South
—	—	1 ◇	4 ♡
Dble	Redble	All pass	

It was the first hand of the rubber and as the cards were being dealt, R.R. eagerly crossexamined his partner about conventions.

"Weak Two or do you prefer the Acol near-game type? You don't mind? Well, neither do I, so let's play both. Roman Blackwood and Neapolitan leads in the first three positions, or am I thinking of something else? Kock-Werner and. . ."

The Rabbit was still in full spate when Papa, having completed the deal, bid 1 ◇. R.R.'s 4 ♡ was a natural reflex, and let it be said at once that a better man than he might have been doubled by a player with the West cards. Allowing two tricks for the Rabbit's declarer value to the defence, the Hog felt, no doubt, that he had plenty to spare. The Walrus, for his part, explained that if he couldn't redouble with 11 points—eight in top cards and three for a singleton—he might as well stop counting.

Psychologically, of course, it is usually a mistake to redouble when the Rabbit is to be declarer. It makes him nervous—that is, even more nervous than usual. But it can work both ways, for when R.R. doesn't know what he is doing, he may, inadvertently, do the right thing.

His mind in a whirl, regretting that he had mentioned Kock-Werner and hoping that the redouble wasn't of the SOS type, the Rabbit momentarily lost his precarious sense of balance and led the club jack against his own contract.

When the jeers had subsided and the card was back in the Rabbit's hand, the Hog led the ◊K, then the six through dummy to be taken by Papa's eight. The Greek's febrile mind ticked loudly. If he continued with the ◊A, it should help to promote a trump in partner's hand. But it was clear from the Rabbit's comic opening that he had a singleton club. He might ruff the ◊A high and park his losing club later on the ◊Q. What if it promoted a trump for H.H.? The defence would have simply gained one trick at the expense of another. And it would be worse still if, at trick three, Papa continued with a low diamond. The Rabbit would discard his club and the Hog would be wasting a trump on a loser.

The way out of the impasse came to Papa in a flash. Nudging the nearest kibitzer in the ribs and winking significantly at the others, he swished the king of clubs in midair. Then he slapped the card down on the table, picked up the Rabbit's lone jack, and shot the deuce of diamonds flamboyantly along the green baize. Having made the best of both worlds, he sat back contentedly to watch the result. The Rabbit ruffed with the eight, and having nothing better to do, drew trumps. As he led the ♡9, his last one, this was the position:

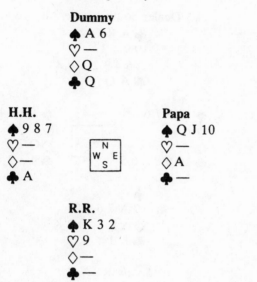

Dummy
♠ A 6
♡ —
◇ Q
♣ Q

H.H.
♠ 9 8 7
♡ —
◇ —
♣ A

Papa
♠ Q J 10
♡ —
◇ A
♣ —

R.R.
♠ K 3 2
♡ 9
◇ —
♣ —

The Hog had to throw a spade to keep his ace of clubs. "Ah well," said the Rabbit, shrugging his shoulders philosophically, "I don't suppose that Papa will discard his ace of clubs." He ditched dummy's ♣ Q and the Greek clinging desperately to the ◇A, was forced to part with a spade. Much to his own surprise, the Rabbit scored his tenth trick with the deuce of spades. To this day he doesn't know how or why.

"Fancy the Hog and Papa discarding so badly," he said to me afterwards. "Only goes to show that even the best players make mistakes."

I thought I heard an impish laugh in the distance. It was probably a bottle of champagne stirring in the ice bucket, but I couldn't help thinking of R.R.'s guardian angel.

The Rabbit Blushes

This was another Rabbit hand submitted to our Committee:

Dealer South—Love All

♠ A K Q 2
♡ 9 4 3
◊ 6 4 3 2
♣ A Q

♠ 10 8 7 6   ♠ J 9 5 4 3
♡ K J 8   ♡ Q 10
◊ —   ◊ Q 7 5
♣ 10 9 8 7 6 5 ♣ 4 3 2

```
    N
  W   E
    S
```

♠ —
♡ A 7 6 5 2
◊ A K J 10 9 8
♣ K J

South	North
1 ◊	1 ♠
2 ♡	4 ◊
4 ♡	4 NT
5 ♡	6 ♣
7 ◊	

It should be said in fairness to the Rabbit that he mistook the Toucan's 6 ♣ for the grand slam force, asking him to bid 7 ◊ if he had two of the three top diamond honours. The Toucan, it transpired later, intended his 6 ♣ to be a 'two-way' bid.

The Rabbit won the opening club lead with the ace, thoughtfully dropping the king to ensure an entry in dummy. Then he led a trump to his ace. When West showed out he counted the trumps. There were a lot of them and he was about to play the king, to drop the queen, when something held him back and he counted again.

"One cannot be too careful," he said to himself *sotto voce* when the recount revealed another trump. Congratulating himself on his unblocking play in clubs, he overtook the jack with the queen, finessed and brought down the ◊Q. Three trumps later he realised to his horror that he had forgotten to cash dummy's spades, and that as his lowest trump was higher than dummy's biggest, there was no way back. Blushing guiltily, with beads of perspiration trickling down his forehead, the Rabbit played his last diamond. As it hit the table, the guardian angel quickly took charge. Every heart, right down to the deuce, turned into a winner.

East blamed West and West blamed East, but never the twain did meet. For how could either fail to keep four spades? East could afford to part with one, though not, of course, with two. Seeing East throw a spade, West was more determined than ever to cling to every one of his. Declarer was marked with one spade at least. Since East had shed one, he could not have left more than three, so it was up to West to look after the spades, leaving his partner to guard the hearts.

"That Rabbit," said Colin bitterly. "He mixes up his conventions, miscounts the trumps, forgets to lose the contract through sheer carelessness and is rewarded for his sins with a grand slam. Any sort of handicap and he would have made overtricks."

Handicapping the Humble Hog

How should we handicap the Hideous Hog, the best player in the club and the most insufferable in the country? That was the main issue before this week's meeting of H.A.C.—the Handicapping Committee of the Griffins Club.

Blinking solemnly, Oscar the Owl, our President, addressed us: "There have been complaints," he said. "For more than a fortnight the Hog has insulted no one, not even the Rabbit. And not only has he been brazenly civil, but he has been apologising unctuously to all and sundry, and more especially to his hated rival, Papa the Greek.

"'Forgive me, Themistocles,' he has been heard saying. 'Of course I should have known that singleton was a false card. It stood out a mile. There's no excuse.' Or again: 'Sorry Papa, I should have steered the contract into your hand. You are the only man in the club who might have made it.'

"The members don't like it," went on Oscar. "It's unnatural.
It's not in the spirit of the game and everyone's suspicious. I don't
blame them."

"The Hog is only trying to keep down his handicap," warned
Colin the Corgi, "but we mustn't let him psyche us, and he's
overdoing it, you know. It's all very well allowing the Walrus to
play two hands in the same rubber, but not being rude to Papa is
positively ostentatious. It's in bad taste. Why, think of that slam
only yesterday. . . ."

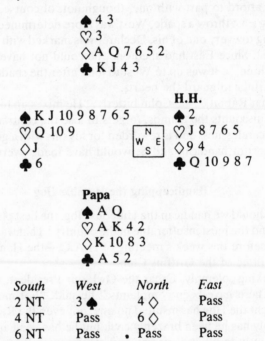

```
                    ♠ 4 3
                    ♡ 3
                    ◇ A Q 7 6 5 2
                    ♣ K J 4 3

                                    H.H.
     ♠ K J 10 9 8 7 6 5            ♠ 2
     ♡ Q 10 9          N           ♡ J 8 7 6 5
     ◇ J            W     E        ◇ 9 4
     ♣ 6               S           ♣ Q 10 9 8 7

                    Papa
                    ♠ A Q
                    ♡ A K 4 2
                    ◇ K 10 8 3
                    ♣ A 5 2
```

South	West	North	East
2 NT	3 ♠	4 ◇	Pass
4 NT	Pass	6 ◇	Pass
6 NT	Pass	Pass	Pass

Papa's opening was on the light side, but it is only fair to say
that he did not realise till later that he was being watched and had
he bid anything else, he would have run a serious risk of ending
up as dummy.

West opened the ◇J. The Greek won in his hand and led a low
club, losing the finesse to the Hog's queen.

Suddenly, with a flourish, H.H. tabled his hand, conceding the contract and congratulating Papa on his brilliance. In loud and ringing tones, so that all could hear, he made a comprehensive statement on how he would lose the rest of the tricks.

"Every card is marked," he began, beaming at us all and especially at the members of the Handicapping Committee. "Papa must have the ♠ A Q. Precisely that, for with the K Q or the Q J, for that matter, my partner would have opened a spade, not a diamond. The ♡ A K are, of course, an integral part of the opening bid. Without them the hand wouldn't add up to more than 19 and a fine, dependable partner like Themistocles Papadoulos wouldn't bid 2 NT on less than 20. But note that he cannot have the ♡ Q, too, for then he would have 12 tricks on top.

"Observe also," went on the Hideous Hog, raising a podgy, pink forefinger, "how skilfully our friend rectified the count with that astute finesse in clubs. What happens next? I lead back partner's suit, of course, but Papa slaps down the ace, lays down the ♣ A K and reels off his six diamonds, leaving three threes in dummy: in spades, hearts, and clubs. In his hand he retains the A K 2 of hearts. Having to keep a club, I must come down to two hearts. My poor partner is threatened by dummy's spade, so he too can retain no more than two hearts. I only wish," concluded the Hog, bowing to the Greek, "that I could have played the hand like that myself."

"A splendid analysis!" murmured one of the junior kibitzers.

Papa turned on him in a flash. "What's splendid about it?" he barked. "Elementary, automatic squeeze. A child of six would see it. Why. . ."

This was too much for the Hog. "What!" he roared. "You really think that I couldn't have beaten you in the usual way? I'm not saying a word about the contract, mind you. There'd be no future in 6 ◇, which is unbeatable, since you wouldn't be playing the hand. But surely even you can see that a heart return from me breaks your silly squeeze to smithereens. A child of five. . ."

"Why, then," interrupted Oscar, "didn't you return a heart?"

The Hog clenched his teeth and gulped. This was no time for

pride. All three members of the Handicapping Committee were present and he reckoned that he played over two thousand rubbers a year at £5 a hundred. Contorting his features into a sickly smile, he replied meekly: "Anno Domini, my dear Oscar. I'm not so young as I used to be. One only sees these things afterwards, when it's too late, I fear."

"It's quite true, you know," said Colin the Corgi. "No one has aged so much as the Hog in the last week or two, since this handicapping idea came up."

The Quickest Card is the Best

A problem of a different order came up before the same meeting of our Committee. A new member had joined the Griffins, and with virtually nothing to go on we had to give him a provisional handicap. This was the only hand which was brought to our attention:

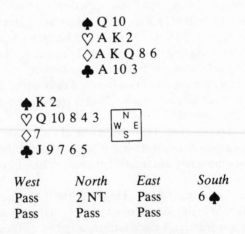

```
              ♠ Q 10
              ♡ A K 2
              ◇ A K Q 8 6
              ♣ A 10 3

  ♠ K 2
  ♡ Q 10 8 4 3      N
  ◇ 7            W     E
  ♣ J 9 7 6 5      S
```

West	North	East	South
Pass	2 NT	Pass	6 ♠
Pass	Pass	Pass	

The new Griffin, sitting West, opened the ◇7. Declarer won in his hand and led the ♠ 3, to which the stranger followed with the deuce. On the strength of that play we had to handicap him.

"A far-sighted defence," said Oscar the Owl. "Declarer is marked with seven spades, if not eight, headed by the ace. But he cannot have the jack, too, for then his play would make no sense. No, he is clearly trying to guard against K J x in one hand. West sees that the defence cannot come to more than one trump trick and that the contract is, therefore, unbeatable unless declarer can be induced to take a wrong view. So he plays low, hoping that declarer will insert dummy's ten and that partner, coming in with the jack, will give him a ruff. To have sorted it all out, West must be pretty good."

C.C. shook his head. "It's far more likely," he said cynically, "that our new member didn't think at all. He just assumed that declarer couldn't have the ace, since he didn't play it, and he was afraid that his king would crash with the bare ace in partner's hand."

Unable to agree amongst ourselves, we decided to consult the Hog. Having no personal interest, he might, for once, speak truthfully.

"Well," said Oscar, after stating the problem, "is our new member good or bad?"

"It's you who are bad, my friends—my *dear* friends," replied H.H., remembering just in time who we were. "Fancy describing a play without mentioning the most important part! How long did it take West to find that deuce of spades? That's the crux of the problem. If he thought at all, even for a couple of seconds, he couldn't hope to induce the wrong guess. Then Colin is right, and he was afraid that partner might have the bare ace. In short, he's a beginner. If he played quickly and smoothly, it was a subtle and daring defence. Then Oscar is right. But don't forget, my dearest friends, that the card you play is sometimes less important than the speed with which you play it. The best defence is often the fastest. And let me tell you," went on the Hideous Hog, warming to the subject and waving aloft Oscar's glass of cognac, "that I owe as much of my success to speed as to technique—that is," he hastily corrected himself, "I did, in my young days. Today, I fear, I have to rely entirely on playing the right cards."

And with a look of abject humility, the Hog put down Oscar's empty glass.

Following a carefully conducted opinion poll among the

Griffins, the handicap project has been abandoned. The figures are revealing. No less than 118% were against it, with only 3% in favour and ½% (the Rueful Rabbit) in the 'Don't Know' category.

The Hideous Hog denies vehemently that he voted more than once. Alternatively, he contends that every member has a moral duty to vote for friends who have not yet been elected and are denied, therefore, the opportunity to vote for themselves.

Chapter 16
LOW-CARD POINTS

"I admit it freely. What's more, I am proud of it," declared the Hideous Hog, despatching the last of the *boeuf Strogonoff*. "Of course I hold better cards than you do, much better cards, but then it's only to be expected. It's part of my system."

"Bah!" hissed the Secretary Bird, his thin bloodless lips curving downward in derision. "Your precious system is all bluff and bluster. To undermine the confidence of your opponents, you persuade them to overrate your play and to underrate their own. And as if that wasn't enough, you pretend to hold better cards, too. All this hocus-pocus is wasted on *me*. I hold just as many aces and kings as you do. Year in and year out, my cards are every bit as good as yours, and we both know it."

The Hog shook his head. "You doubtless hold as many aces and kings as I do, but your cards can never be as good as mine. Never. Measure them in points if you like, and you will soon see it."

Looking more than ever like a Secretary Bird, the Emeritus Professor of Bio-Sophistry untwined his long, wiry legs, a sure sign that he was searching for a devastating retort.

"You want to know why. . ." began the Hog.

"I don't," hissed S.B., "not in the least."

"Very well then," continued the Hog, "I'll tell you. After all, it's not a secret. Everyone knows that we start with the same number of high-card points, though mine, of course, go further than yours. But I hold *low*-card points, too, and you don't. That's the difference between us. There was a good example last night in the weekly pairs at the Unicorn. You must remember this board."

S.B. Loses a Deuce

As he spoke, the Hog neatly abstracted a page from a handsome volume which was lying around, and jotted down a hand:

Dealer West—N/S Vulnerable

♠ 10 3 2
♡ A K 6 5 4
◇ 9 3
♣ A K 9

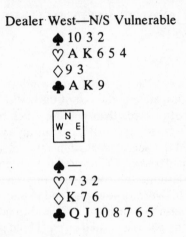

♠ —
♡ 7 3 2
◇ K 7 6
♣ Q J 10 8 7 6 5

"At my table the bidding was:

West	North	East	South
1 ♠	Dble	4 ♠	5 ♣

"I believe," went on H.H., "that you, too, were sitting South and that, like me, you reached a contract of 5 ♣. Distributional values apart, you had 10 high-card points yourself and you found 14 in dummy, making a grand total of 24. Am I right?"

"You had more, of course," scoffed the Secretary Bird.

"Naturally," replied the Hog "which is why I made the contract while you didn't."

"They must have chucked it at you," retorted S.B. "Against good defence it's not on."

"No—that is, not the way you played it," agreed the Hog. "But please don't interrupt," he added severely as the Secretary Bird hissed disapproval. "I know exactly what you did, even though I was at the next table. Presumably your West made the same lead

as mine, the ♠ 8 to East's ace. You ruffed and led a heart at once
to dummy's king. Then, after two rounds of trumps, you led a
second heart, hoping that West would produce the queen. Had
he done so, you would have ducked, setting up dummy's hearts
without letting in East. Unfortunately, West couldn't oblige. He
followed first with the ♡ 10, then with the ♡ J. So you won with
the king and played a third round of hearts, hoping that West had
started with three hearts and would have to take the trick. But
West, it so happens, had been dealt a doubleton. East came in
and promptly shot a diamond through your gizzard, and that put
paid to you."

"Ducking wouldn't have helped in the least," protested S.B.
"East knew his stuff. He would have overtaken East's ♡ 10 or ♡ J
with his queen and he would have played a diamond through my
king, just the same."

"True," agreed H.H., "but you shouldn't have given him the
chance."

"And how was I to stop him?" asked S.B., stamping his foot in
exasperation.

"By playing a spade from dummy instead of a heart from your
hand. That's all," replied the Hideous Hog.

Everyone tried to look unconcerned. The Rabbit tittered. The
Owl hooted. The Toucan concurred.

"Since you all look so mystified, I'd better explain," said H.H.
"At trick two you cross to dummy with a trump and lead the ♠ 2.
East may well play the ♠ 4. . ."

"So what!?" hissed the Secretary Bird.

"So you throw a heart, knowing that since the four is the lowest
spade out, West must overtake. Now, assuming a 3–2 break, you
can set up the hearts without letting in East to play a diamond
through you."

"Is that what happened at your table?" asked the Rueful
Rabbit.

"Not quite," replied the Hog. "East played the five of spades,
not the four, so I had to ruff. When, however, West followed with
the ♠ 4, I tried again crossing to dummy with a trump to lead the
♠ 3. East produced the six, the lowest remaining spade. Since

West couldn't avoid overtaking it, I threw a heart in perfect
safety. These were the four hands:"

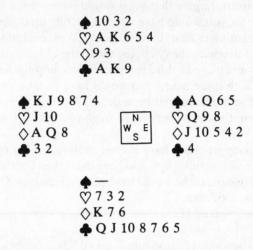

♠ 10 3 2
♡ A K 6 5 4
◇ 9 3
♣ A K 9

♠ K J 9 8 7 4   ♠ A Q 6 5
♡ J 10   ♡ Q 9 8
◇ A Q 8   ◇ J 10 5 4 2
♣ 3 2   ♣ 4

♠ —
♡ 7 3 2
◇ K 7 6
♣ Q J 10 8 7 6 5

"Very lucky," said the Secretary Bird. "What would you have
done, I should like to know, had West retained that ♠ 4?"

"In the last resort I could have played the hearts towards
dummy, as you did," answered H.H., "but I don't like last
resorts, so I gave myself an extra chance of keeping out East.
West, of course, had no reason to cling on to his lowest spade. He
probably thought that I was performing some sort of elimination
and followed naturally. The crux of the hand," concluded H.H.,
"was to exploit the potential of those two little spades."

"Lucky, just the same, to have found them in dummy," persisted S.B.

"Very lucky," agreed the Hog. "I was, in fact, twice as lucky as
you were, for unless I am mistaken, your dummy had the ♠ 3 but
not the two."

"But surely," objected R.R., "if you sat in the same positions
you must have had the same dummies. I mean, even, I, er,
usually. . ."

"Don't you believe it!" said the Hog with a malevolent look at
S.B. "The Professor, I rather think, lost the ♠ 2, yes, just like

that. Not realising its importance, he followed with it to West's opening lead, didn't you, Professor?"

"You mean. . ." began the Rabbit.

"I do," affirmed the Hog. "He should have played the ♠ 10. What's the use of having precious cards, like the two and the three, if you don't know what to do with them?"

A Case of Promotion

Tearing out another page from the book before him, the Hog wrote down this hand:

♠ J 10 9 5
♡ 7 6 5 4
◇ K 10
♣ K 10 9

```
  N
W   E
  S
```

♠ —
♡ A 10 3
◇ A Q J 8 7 6
♣ A Q J 3

"Against 6 ◇, West opened a small trump. This was the bidding:

South	North
2 ◇	2 NT
3 ♣	3 ◇
3 ♡	4 ♣
5 ♣	6 ◇

"We played this board in our last set," went on the Hog, "and I noticed that we were the only two pairs to reach the slam and. . ."

"A hopeless contract!" broke in the Secretary Bird. "My

partner thought that we needed tops and was shooting wildly. The odds against bringing off the slam were over a thousand to one."

"Impossible," rejoined the Hog, "there can be no odds of more than a thousand to one so late at night. A revoke is always a better chance than that. But on this particular hand, after the trump lead, the odds clearly favour declarer."

The Hog looked with satisfaction at the raised eyebrows around him.

"Perhaps you transformed your ♡ 5 into the king," sneered S.B.

"No," replied the Hog. "I transformed the ♠ 5 into the ♠ 8. It came to the same thing."

While perplexed looks were exchanged round the table, the Hog scored two easy overtricks in *crêpes Suzette*.

"That slam," he resumed, putting down someone's glass of Château d'Yquem, "you would have no trouble in playing it if dummy's spades were the J 10 9 8, would you?"

All agreed hastily.

"You would play for divided honours, wouldn't you?" coaxed the Hog.

"Naturally," agreed the Rabbit, wondering what it meant.

"If East has two of the three tops," pursued H.H., "you can't go wrong. You lead the ♠ 8 and unless East covers, you throw a heart. Then, going back to dummy, you play the ♠ 9, all set to throw your other heart. This time, East covers, of course, so you ruff, cross to dummy and repeat the process with the ♠ 10. Again East must cover, and again you ruff, setting up the ♠ J for your twelfth trick.

"There's one serious snag," warned the Hog, pointing a fat, pink forefinger at S.B. "That ♠ 8 you need so badly isn't there. The nearest approach to it is the five and it's a poor imitation, soon quelled by the six or seven without requiring the services of the ace, king or queen. It won't do. To put things right, pretend that the five is the eight. Promote it mentally and play accordingly.

"What happens?" asked H.H. "Why, half the time East will

believe you, for unless he has the ♠ 8 himself he will place you with it. Nothing could be more natural. And even if he can see the eight in his own hand, is he likely to play it from a holding headed by the A K—or the A Q, if it comes to that? Surely not."

"Any moment," chipped in the Emeritus Professor, while the Hog was looking for a glass, "you'll be telling us that this ridiculous slam is an even-money chance."

"Far better," the Hog assured him a gulp later. "Since West opened a trump he can hardly have the ♠ A K or even the K Q. In fact, after a bidding sequence advertising a two-suiter, he might well have led the ace from the A Q. So you see, East is pretty certain to have two of the three tops in spades. Everything is in declarer's favour—except that eight, and many players," added the Hog, with a look of disdain at S.B., as he uncovered the East–West hands, "don't bother about such trifles."

This was the deal in full:

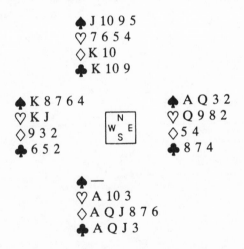

"View it objectively," pleaded H.H. "Don't let a bottom affect your judgment. One more couldn't have made much difference to you, and you must agree that once the 3 NT mark is passed, the slam is mandatory. A minor suit game rarely leads to a good score in a pairs event. There are exceptions, of course. Let me show you..." The Hog broke off to leaf through the book before him in search of another blank page. Finding none, he handed it to the Emeritus Professor of Bio-Sophistry. "It's yours, I believe," he said politely.

"Vandal!" cried S.B., the tufts of hair over his ears bristling with anger. "You've been scrawling your beastly hands on pages torn out of my *Iliad*!"

"Is that what it is?" asked the Hog with a chuckle. "No wonder those hands were all Greek to you. Ha! ha! ha!"

Chapter 17
THE RABBIT MUTINIES

"I assure you that we had the blues. I know for certain, because I picked them myself. I had a reason. And it's so unlucky, so very unlucky to change packs in the middle of a rubber."

There was a note of entreaty in the Rabbit's voice as he pleaded with his partner, the Hideous Hog, who continued, unmoved, to deal the red cards.

The Rueful Rabbit seemed genuinely upset. His hands trembled and a bead of perspiration stood on his forehead. No one, however, paid much attention to him. The Walrus was trying to recount a cruel experience which had befallen him earlier in the evening. The Emeritus Professor of Bio-Sophistry was not listening to anyone. He was too deeply engrossed in hating the Hog.

"Do stop dealing," begged the Rabbit. "I have been lucky all day. Now everything will go wrong, every finesse, every card, please. . ."

But it was already too late. The Hog had completed the deal and fixing a maleficent eye on the gardenia in his partner's buttonhole, he addressed him scornfully: "I do not doubt your luck," he said, "and I know no one who needs it more than you do. But you'll be luckier still if you concentrate on the face of the cards rather than on their backs, unless of course, both sides look much alike to you. 1 ♠."

Reluctantly, with foreboding, the Rabbit accepted the situation. Yet it was so wanton, he felt, to court bad luck deliberately, and the message in 'The Stars Speak' in the *Gazette* that morning had been quite unmistakable. He could see the words distinctly in his mind's eye: 'Virgo: 24th Aug–22nd Sept. Resist change. Be wary of your associates. After nightfall things may not be what they seem. Lucky colour, blue. Lucky flower, gardenia.' Could anything be clearer?

Giving up all hope of finding an audience for his hard-luck

story, Walter the Walrus passed. Then, being a careful man, he
sorted his cards and studied them closely.

Rarely had I seen the Rueful Rabbit look so angry. The Hog
was a fine player, and no one could deny his right to be rude, but
there was no justification for switching the cards. Skill did not
come into it. The Rabbit unburdened himself at length to me
afterwards. At the time, all he said was: "3 NT." And he
looked defiantly round the table as he said it.

The Hog's small beady eyes narrowed perceptibly. The
Emeritus Professor of Bio-Sophistry blinked behind his pince-
nez. Even Walter the Walrus looked less vacant than usual. For it
was an unwritten law that to avoid the risk of having to play the
hand, the Rabbit must not bid notrumps. To do so deliberately,
without even trying to steer the contract into the Hog's capable
hands, was an act of blatant insubordination.

Three Wrongs Make a Right

This was the deal:

Dealer North—Love All

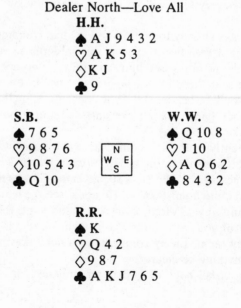

H.H.
♠ A J 9 4 3 2
♡ A K 5 3
◇ K J
♣ 9

S.B.
♠ 7 6 5
♡ 9 8 7 6
◇ 10 5 4 3
♣ Q 10

W.W.
♠ Q 10 8
♡ J 10
◇ A Q 6 2
♣ 8 4 3 2

R.R.
♠ K
♡ Q 4 2
◇ 9 8 7
♣ A K J 7 6 5

West	North	East	South
—	1 ♠	Pass	3 NT

I expected H.H. to call 4 ♠ over the Rabbit's 3 NT, but after looking intently at his partner, the Hog thought better of it. Clearly the Rabbit was in an ugly mood, and might go on calling notrumps forever out of sheer spite. The Hog snarled and passed.

The Secretary Bird's opening was a small diamond, on which R.R. threw the seven from his hand.

"It's dummy to play," all called at once.

"Does it matter?" replied the Rabbit bitterly. "Every card is bound to be wrong, anyway, so why worry?"

As the Walrus produced the ace-queen over dummy's king-jack, the Rabbit looked positively pleased. His black prophecies were being fulfilled.

The defence went on with diamonds, S.B. having started with 10 5 4 3. After following for three rounds, the Rabbit discarded a club from his hand. From dummy he threw two spades.

After taking the first four tricks in diamonds, S.B. led the ♠ 7. The Rabbit played the jack from the table and captured W.W.'s queen with his king.

Still nodding to himself and seeming to revel in misfortune, the Rabbit attacked hearts. Twice he played from the wrong hand but the final, if fortuitous order of tricks was ace, king and queen. When, on the third round, the Walrus parted with the ♣ 2, R.R. smiled mirthlessly. How could hearts break, he seemed to be saying, after the packs had been switched so brutally?

Once more he tried to lead from the wrong hand, but with a rapier-like thrust of his pencil, the Hideous Hog stopped him from grabbing the ♣ 9.

"It makes no difference," snapped the exasperated Rabbit. "No finesse can succeed anyway."

On the ♣ A, S.B. dropped the ten. To the king he followed with the queen. R.R. emitted a soft squeak, in which pleasure had the edge over bitterness. He cashed his ♣ J and threw his last two clubs on the table.

"There," he said triumphantly, "two down, but I ask you to

note that every card was wrong. The ◇ A Q were over the K J, both black queens were over the jacks, and, of course, the hearts did not break. These are facts and. . ."

"Despite your best endeavours," interrupted the Hog, "you have made the contract. No more clubs are out, Walter having discarded one, and since no one can win a trick from you, there is no way in which you can lose one—not even playing with the red pack."

"4 ♠ is cold," said someone.

"Curious hand," observed Oscar the Owl. "If the hearts are played correctly, East is genuinely squeezed, but not knowing the position, declarer takes the club finesse and goes down. To make the wrong contract declarer misplays two suits and executes, unintentionally, a pseudo-squeeze in place of a true one. Three wrongs make a right."

"I think," said Peregrine the Penguin, "that R.R. alone could have brought home this contract."

"Or got into it," added Oscar.

"No, no," said the Rabbit modestly, casting down his long eyelashes, but his delicate nose twitched and his long ears, tingling with pleasure, proclaimed to the world that he felt deeply flattered.

The Rueful Rabbit had another secret reason for rejoicing. Unnoticed by anyone, he had deftly switched the cards, and now the Walrus was dealing with the red pack.

S.B. Makes Ready for the Kill

W.W. opened 1 ♣. The Rabbit came in with 3 ♠, and the Secretary Bird promptly doubled. I moved over to sit between North and West. Their hands were:

Dealer East—Game All

H.H.
♠ Q 8 7
♡ Q 6 5 4 3
◇ 2
♣ J 9 8 7

S.B.   **W.W.**
♠ A J
♡ J 10 9 8
◇ A K Q 3
♣ 4 3 2

R.R.

It was difficult to blame S.B. for doubling, especially in view of
the vulnerability, but any doubts he had must have been speedily
set at rest when the Hog, in a firm and confident voice, called
3 NT.

Two inexperienced kibitzers were visibly shaken. They did not
know H.H. Accustomed as I was to his methods, I was reason-
ably certain of what was in his mind.

It looked very much as if the Walrus had one spade or none.
With a freakish hand, he might well be tempted to bid on, and all
would then be well. And even if that absurd Walrus had the
impudence to double, H.H. could surely expect to make more
tricks in notrumps than the Rabbit could hope to collect in any
contract. In a critical situation risks had to be taken, and H.H
knew precisely when and how to take them. More often than not,
they came off.

Alas, it was not to be. The Walrus doubled in a voice of
thunder, and then the impossible came to pass. The Rabbit
rescued the Hog! Just as if it were the most ordinary thing in the
world, he called 4 ♠. Of course this was without precedent.
Transcending the extreme bounds of insubordination, it
amounted to nothing less than mutiny.

I looked at R.R. His face was flushed, and a moist lock of

ash-grey hair had fallen over his forehead. There was a wild look
in his eyes, and his nostrils quivered. Penguin's words 'only R.R.
could have brought home the contract', mingling with the fumes
of cherry brandy, had completely turned the poor Rabbit's head.

Hissing voluptuously, the Secretary Bird doubled and made
ready for the kill. The Hog grunted, gritted his teeth and passed.
What else was there to do with a partner who had taken leave of
his feeble senses?

This had been the sequence:

West	North	East	South
—	—	1 ♣	3 ♠
Dble	3 NT	Dble	4 ♠
Dble			

The opening was the ◇ K. Then, taking one look at dummy,
S.B. decided to attack its ruffing value. To the second trick he led
the ace of trumps on which, with a cry of anguish, Walter the
Walrus dropped the king. It began to look as if the Rabbit might
get out of it for a mere 500 or at worst 800. I walked round to see
the other hands. This was the deal:

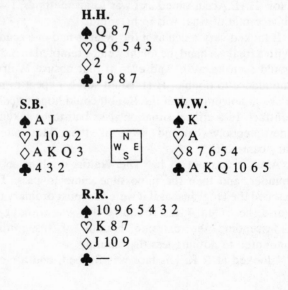

H.H.
♠ Q 8 7
♡ Q 6 5 4 3
◇ 2
♣ J 9 8 7

S.B.
♠ A J
♡ J 10 9 2
◇ A K Q 3
♣ 4 3 2

W.W.
♠ K
♡ A
◇ 8 7 6 5 4
♣ A K Q 10 6 5

R.R.
♠ 10 9 6 5 4 3 2
♡ K 8 7
◇ J 10 9
♣ —

Looking resentfully at his partner, the Secretary Bird continued with the ♠ J. The Rabbit won the trick on the table and tried a heart, which East took with his lone ace. The ♣ K followed. The Rabbit ruffed. Then he trumped a diamond in dummy and, returning to his hand with the ♡ K, played out his trumps one by one.

As spade followed spade, the Secretary Bird, looking wilder and fiercer behind his pince-nez, registered increasing distress. The final turn of the screw found him in this position. What could he possibly spare on that last trump?

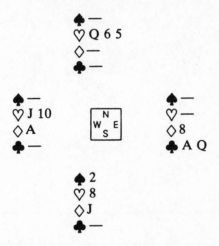

No one was more surprised than R.R. to find that dummy's two little hearts materialised into tricks. Nodding sympathetically, he took it all with good grace, for no one knew better than he how unlucky one could be with one's discards. But it was refreshing, for once, not to be at the receiving end, and he beamed with pleasure.

"I hate those close doubles," roared the Walrus. "We had between us 31 points and three tens. Surely we could have made game ourselves or. . ."

"Or even a grand slam in diamonds, clubs or notrumps," cut in the Hideous Hog with a rhythmic purr-like snort. He had added

up the score and was his old self again. "But admit it, my dear
Walter," he went on, directing at the Walrus a jaunty, malevolent look, "my 3 NT fixed you completely. Ha! ha! Needless to
say," he added turning to S.B., "I would have taken it out into
4 ♠ myself had my partner not done it for me. Once I'd persuaded
you to abandon your grand slam in favour of presenting us with a
game, my work was done. Ha! ha! But never mind, Professor.
Your turn will come—one day."

Reflecting that every card had been right for him, the Rabbit
looked affectionately at the blue pack.

Chapter 18

BIDDING WITH THE ODDS

There was time for at least a bottle before dinner, and the Hog was in a philosophic mood.

"In bridge, as in every important sphere of life," he declared, "horse sense is to mathematics as three is to one. Yes, yes, I know someone said it before—Socrates or Napoleon, or I may have said it myself—but it's true for all that. Odds and percentages in the play correspond to conventions and systems in the bidding. They take the place of thinking, which is why they are so popular."

"But you believe in odds and percentages yourself," protested the Rueful Rabbit. "Why, I've often heard you say that when poor Walter bids a slam against you, the penalty double is preferable to the Lightner, because there are only four suits, so it's no more than three to one against partner leading the right one anyway; whereas it is ten to one at least against the Walrus making twelve tricks on any given hand. And don't you always say that if there are two ways to play a hand the odds are three to one that I, that, er, Walter, will find the wrong one? Isn't that a question of odds?"

"True," agreed the Hog, "but they are human odds, that is, if you can call that Walrus human. And talking of the Walrus, here's a percentage hand for you."

Shutting Out Partner

The Hog scribbled on a serviette:

♠ A K Q 2
♡ A 6
◇ A K Q
♣ A 6 4 2

```
  N
W   E
  S
```

♠ 4 3
♡ K Q J 9 8
◇ J 10 8
♣ Q 5 3

South	North
Pass	2 ♣
2 ◇	3 NT
6 ♡	6 NT
7 ♡	

"I was South and against my 7 ♡, West led a trump. Proceed," commanded the Hog.

"But how could you bid 7 ♡?" asked the Rabbit. "You might have been missing an ace."

"I was playing with that Walrus," explained the Hog, "and it was a straightforward routine bidding sequence.

"I can't make the first-round response of 2 NT in case partner has nothing in spades. My 2◇ is, therefore, a waiting bid, prepared for all eventualities. If partner's suit is spades, I'll be the first to bid notrumps. If, by a coincidence, he too has hearts, he won't be able to insist on them without my support and I shall, of course, keep my own counsel. Should he have solid diamonds, I shall play the hand since I bid the suit first. So again, all is well. The only danger, needless to say, is that partner will bid notrumps before I do, but my hearts are good enough to stand it. Anyway," concluded H.H., "whether you like it or not, I succeeded in shutting him out, and the contract is 7 ♡."

"We seem to be one trick short," observed Oscar.

"Then the answer must be a squeeze," said the Toucan. "It's in every book and there's a formula. . ."

"Yes," agreed the Rabbit, nodding vigorously, "and the first thing is to rectify the count, to concede the inevitable loser, then . . ."

"The difficulty with a squeeze," pointed out O.O., "is that if we at once try to cash dummy's three diamonds, we may get a ruff, and if we first draw trumps and then cross to dummy for the diamonds, we'll end up in the wrong hand for squeezing."

"Leave a trump or two in your hand," suggested the Rabbit hopefully.

"Wouldn't help," replied the Owl. "I couldn't get back from dummy without ruffing that fourth spade and that, of course, is a vital menace."

"What sort of squeeze had you in mind, Oscar?" asked H.H.

"If West has the ♣ K and four or five spades. . ." began O.O.

"He hasn't," interrupted the Hog, "so even if you manage to get back to your squeeze card without killing one of your menaces, it won't do you much good. These were the four hands:"

"I wish you had left him in 6 NT. These rescues never pay," said the Rabbit sombrely.

"Come along with me," invited H.H., raising R.R.'s glass in a friendly gesture, "and I'll show you. The first three cards to play should all be aces. After the $\heartsuit$ A at trick one, you follow with the $\diamondsuit$ A, then the $\clubsuit$ A. Now you reel off the trumps, all of them, throwing dummy's king and queen of diamonds. This releases the $\diamondsuit$ J 10, which come next. From dummy you discard clubs, leaving the $\spadesuit$ A K Q 2 as the last four cards. Your own four, when you lead the $\diamondsuit$ 10, are the $\spadesuit$ 4 3 and the $\clubsuit$ Q 5. What can East do? To retain his four spades and the $\clubsuit$ K he needs to keep five cards, and he must come down to four. Mind you," added the Hog, "it would be just the same if the East–West hands were reversed. The squeeze is on either way."

"It's still an indefensible contract," said O.O. severely. "You threw away a certain small slam in notrumps in favour of a dubious grand slam in hearts."

"A very superficial analysis," replied the Hog. "Because you see twelve tricks, you assume that the Walrus would make a small slam. You forget that W.W. plus 12 equals 11. Get your equations right, my dear Oscar. On the one side are the odds against my little Vienna Coup and on the other the odds against the Walrus not blocking the hearts. Which is the more likely?"

"Didn't Walter resent your contemptuous attitude?" asked Timothy the Toucan, who had been so often at the receiving end.

"Of course not," replied the Hog. "He accepted the slam bonus with good grace, and though he didn't like to lose his 150 honours, he was big enough to admit that I couldn't be sure from the bidding that he had them."

A Subtle Signal

Reassured by the sound of a popping cork, the Hog cleared his throat and turned to Oscar: "So you wouldn't bid a grand slam without making sure that no ace was missing? How about missing two aces then, or better still, three aces?

"And that reminds me of another grand slam," chortled the Hog, "which, I confess, gave me a lot of pleasure."

"Something disagreeable happened to Papa?" enquired the Owl.

The Hog nodded. "And not only to Papa," he went on with an air of unmistakable satisfaction, "but also to that young friend of Colin's, the one with a long neck and a llama-like look of condescension which, I am sure, he wears when he's asleep. You know, the chap who needs a haircut and thinks that all things worth while, from sex to suit signals, were discovered by the underthirties. He was Papa's partner and. . ."

The arrival of caviar and smoked-salmon canapés caused a temporary diversion.

"I'm getting hoarse. You watched the hand," went on H.H., turning to me. "Tell them about it."

I remembered the deal well.

Larry the Llama, as he came to be known, looked down on simple, straightforward methods as being fit only for the older generation. With all the modern treatments, gadgets and conventions at their fingertips, younger men, he believed, could do a lot better.

The Hog cut the Rabbit and this was the very first hand I followed from a seat between R.R. and Papa:

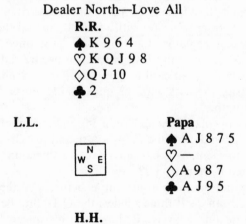

Dealer North—Love All
R.R.
♠ K 9 6 4
♡ K Q J 9 8
♢ Q J 10
♣ 2

L.L.

Papa
♠ A J 8 7 5
♡ —
♢ A 9 8 7
♣ A J 9 5

H.H.

West	North	East	South
—	1 ♠	Pass	2 ♡
Pass	3 ♡	3 NT	4 ♡
5 ♣	5 ♡	6 ♣	7 ♡
Pass	Pass	Dble	

The first part of the auction made sense. The second part did not. The Rabbit's 1 ♠ was a prepared bid which would allow him to show both majors economically. At his first turn Papa understandably passed, but the mention of hearts transformed the situation and, seizing the initiative, he entered the fray boldly with 3 NT, calling for partner's minor.

While the players reviewed the bidding, I tried hard to visualise the Hog's hand. Nothing he could hold fitted the bidding and no combination of the outstanding cards, so far as I could see, would give him the remotest chance of making his contract.

I was still wondering what made him get into it when Larry the Llama produced the two of spades.

The Greek explained to us later what was running through his mind as he took stock of an admittedly unusual situation. The Hog clearly had a very freakish hand with a void somewhere, probably with two voids. Partner's deuce looked very much like the fourth highest from Q 10 3 2, in which case going up with the ace would present declarer with a trick. If, on the other hand, the deuce was a singleton, the Hog must have three spades and therefore an inescapable loser, whatever the Greek did. The jack was clearly the right card to play, and Papa played it.

Capturing the trick with the queen, H.H. crossed to dummy with a trump.

The Llama played the ♣ 10, leaving eight trumps for declarer. Next the Hog detached dummy's ♠ 6, and the Greek was once more in torment. Was partner's deuce a singleton, after all, or had he led it from 10 3 2?

In the end the same argument as before won the day. If the Hog had been dealt three spades, the Q 10 3 to be precise, he would lose one anyway. If, however, his queen had been a singleton, going up with the ace would cost a trick. Thereupon

Papa played the ♠ 7. The Hog won the trick with the ten, while Larry the Llama, nonchalantly, as if he hadn't a care in the world, followed with the ♠ 3. Nothing in his manner showed that he was placing on the table a card that he didn't, that he couldn't possibly have, the very antithesis, as it were, of a revoke.

Unable to bear the suspense any longer, I walked round the table to see the other hands.

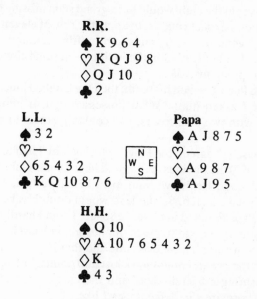

R.R.
♠ K 9 6 4
♡ K Q J 9 8
◇ Q J 10
♣ 2

L.L.
♠ 3 2
♡ —
◇ 6 5 4 3 2
♣ K Q 10 8 7 6

Papa
♠ A J 8 7 5
♡ —
◇ A 9 8 7
♣ A J 9 5

H.H.
♠ Q 10
♡ A 10 7 6 5 4 3 2
◇ K
♣ 4 3

While Papa spluttered with rage, uttering terrible imprecations in Greek, the Hog went back to dummy with a trump and led the ♠ K. Papa covered and H.H. ruffed. With another trump the Hog returned to the table and, after throwing his ◇K on the ♠ 9, led the ◇Q. Papa went up with the ace, but it made no difference. Dummy's fifth trump provided another entry, allowing the Hog to park his two club losers on the ◇ J 10.

"Why, why, why," cried Papa, "did you lead the two from the three-two? Why did you invent this atrocity? What have I ever done to you? Why. . ."

"Because," interposed L.L., with the good-humoured

indulgence that the young vouchsafe to their elders, "the double of a freely bid grand slam is Lightner-indicating that you would ruff a spade. I am sure that you must be familiar with this ancient convention. My deuce was, therefore, an unmistakable suit signal, calling for a club return.

"I could hardly expect," went on the young Llama, "that this gentleman, whom you described to me just now as the second-best player in the club, would bid a grand slam missing three aces. And I didn't expect you, sir, to apply the rule of eleven. I thought that had gone out with trams and muffin men and spongebag trousers. Evidently it's still the in thing—in some circles," added L.L., dropping his voice.

While Papa gnashed his teeth, the Hog laughed loud and long.

Later I asked him: "What possessed you to jump to 7 ♡? Surely, with two club losers, you couldn't expect to make even 6 ♡."

"Precisely," agreed the Hog, "which is why I had to bid seven. Against 6 ♡ the obvious lead would have been a club. But if I bid a grand slam, freely, without even being pushed, I obviously couldn't have a club. So the lead would doubtless be a heart or else, if Papa doubled in a rage, a spade. I could hardly guess that we should have quite so much duplication in hearts, that what's-his-name wouldn't have even one and that Papa would have the ♠ A. In the event, I might have lost 500 points, but against that I was ensuring a friendly lead and the chance to make a grand slam. Those are the percentages I like.

"I didn't know, of course," went on H.H., looking sternly at the Rabbit, "that my partner, having opened on a minimum, was bidding gaily at the five level on an aceless hand. Never mind," added the Hog, as the Rabbit was about to mumble something; "I am not vindictive. But be more careful in future. Next time Papa may have all four aces, and then even I may find some difficulty in making thirteen tricks."

Horse sense, as the Hog is never tired of telling us, should always come before science. It's the cornerstone of his philosophy, and he was pursuing the theme once more over dinner the following night.

Chapter 19

THE SWINGS AND THE ROUNDABOUT

"Why do you suppose, my friends, that you play so badly?" asked the Hideous Hog, despatching the last of the game pie. "I'll tell you. It is because too much duplicate has instilled in you a false sense of shame, a prudish dread of bad contracts. That's why you neither make them nor break them. Unlike the robust rubber bridge player, who doesn't care how he wins, you've acquired a guilt complex. Yes, most of you would rather go down in a good grand slam than make a bad one. That's what comes of substituting a flurry of matchpoints for good, honest money.

"What is a bad grand slam, anyway?" demanded the Hog rhetorically, waving aloft a glass of Vosne Romanée.

Oscar the Owl, our Senior Kibitzer, blinked. Then he blinked again. He didn't like to commit himself beyond that.

"I fully understand that you would rather not admit it," pursued the Hideous Hog, "but you think it is a crime to be in seven missing an ace, don't you? And so it is, of course, if opponents lead it. But what if they don't and you make the slam? Is it still a crime? Of course not. It's a mere sin, morally reprehensible, no doubt, but worth 1,000 points or 1,500, according to vulnerability. And why should opponents invariably lead the right card? Is that what your partners always do?" scoffed H.H.

In a swift, combined movement, he emptied his glass and raised the bottle to refill it. A gulp or two later he resumed: "Unlucky leads and bad breaks wreck many a sound contract. To redress the balance, a fair share of poor ones must be brought home. What's more," went on the Hideous Hog, pointing an accusing finger at the waiter, who had brought the bill, "the true artist is always modest. He doesn't insist on the best contract. The second-best is good enough for him, and the third-best and sometimes the fourth. I showed you a couple of good aceless slams the other day. Here's another."

As he spoke, H.H. searched his pockets. Frowning, he went through his wallet. Then he looked around him. "I beg of you," he said to the Rueful Rabbit, seeing him draw out his chequebook to pay the bill, "lend me a cheque form. No, no, I insist."

Dumbfounded, R.R. allowed the chequebook to be snatched from him. O.O. gave up his fountain pen without a murmur. Peregrine the Penguin opened his mouth and forgot to close it. That the Hog, always so distrait on such occasions, should forcibly take over the bill was an experience without precedent.

The Piscatorial Coup

The Hog's figures were big and bold. "There you are," he said, handing the cheque to Oscar. "You are East."

These were the two hands written on the back of the cheque form:

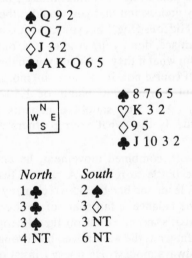

♠ Q 9 2
♡ Q 7
♢ J 3 2
♣ A K Q 6 5

```
      N
    W   E
      S
```

♠ 8 7 6 5
♡ K 3 2
♢ 9 5
♣ J 10 3 2

North	South
1 ♣	2 ♠
3 ♣	3 ♢
3 ♠	3 NT
4 NT	6 NT

"West leads the ♣ 9. Declarer goes up with the ace, following with the ♣ 8 himself, and at trick two he leads dummy's ♣ 6. Go on from there."

No one said anything. Seeing us study the bidding, H.H. recapitulated. "North opens 1 ♣ and South forces with 2 ♣. Over the 3 ♣ rebid he calls 3 ♢, and after hearing the 3 ♠ preference bid, he is willing to settle for 3 NT. North, however, makes an effort and South shoots the slam."

The Penguin was the first to speak. "Looks fishy," he said. "Why should declarer so tamely give up a club trick?"

"I don't return a diamond," declared the Rabbit firmly.

"Why?' asked H.H.

"Because that's what I'd do," explained the Rueful Rabbit, "so it can't be right and therefore I don't do it, if you see what I mean."

Colin the Corgi and the Secretary Bird, who were sitting at the next table, joined in the discussion.

"The ♡ K for me," said Colin flippantly. No one asked him why, so he told us: "Just as it's usually the kindly old lady who commits the murder, from some obscure motive revealed on the last page but one, so when H.H. sets you a problem you look for the most unlikely solution, and could anything be more unlikely than the ♡ K?"

"May one enquire," asked the Emeritus Professor, smirking graciously, "what card declarer played to the second trick—if it's not a secret, of course."

"The usual movement at bridge being clockwise," retorted the Hog, "perhaps you would tell us first, Professor, which card you played as East."

"The jack and ten are, I believe, equal," hissed back S.B.; "but since it's so important to you, let's say that I played the ten."

"Declarer plays the ♡ 8," said H.H. "Your turn, Professor."

"I return the ♠ 6," announced S.B., "a delicate false-card, revealing nothing, helping no one."

"I play back a club," vouchsafed the Owl, suddenly coming to life. "After all, he's got to make those clubs. Meanwhile, I'll watch his discards."

The Hideous Hog sat back happily. "You are all wrong," he announced. "Every one of you."

"Since between us we have exhausted every possibility, one of us must be right," insisted O.O.

"On the contrary," declared H.H., "you've all missed the point of the hand." Carefully emptying his glass before picking up mine, he continued: "P.P. was the only one with a clue. At least he noted the fishy side, the, er . . ."

"The piscatorial aspect of declarer's play," put in Colin.

"Exactly," agreed the Hog, "why should declarer so readily give up a club trick? And why the *second* club trick? Obviously he had an unavoidable club loser and, to have been sure of that, he must have had a singleton himself. That is the first point. The second is that he clearly needed four club tricks for his contract. But that still doesn't explain why he decided to lose the second club, rather than the first or the third or. . ."

"Rectifying the count for a squeeze?" hazarded the Rabbit.

"Then, surely, he would have ducked the opening lead. No, no." went on the Hog, "there must be some better reason and if you weren't all so shocked by the mere thought of bad contracts, you would have guessed it long ago. The only possible explanation is that declarer is missing an ace—which isn't so unlikely, anyway, seeing that the slam was bid quantitatively. Of course, declarer doesn't know which defender has that ace, but if he ducks the ♣ 9 his fate is sealed either way. Should East have the ace he will overtake the nine and cash it. Should the ace be with West, East will play low. By winning the first trick and thrusting the second on East, declarer doubles his chances of survival, for now, unless East has the missing ace, he cannot tell which suit to return. And that is why," concluded the Hog, putting down my glass, "East should play *low* to the second trick. He should know that his partner has both the missing ace, and above all, that vital card, the ♣ 7." We looked at the four hands:

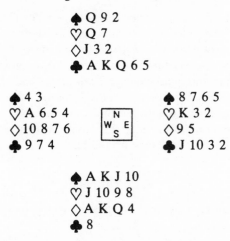

♠ Q 9 2
♡ Q 7
◇ J 3 2
♣ A K Q 6 5

♠ 4 3
♡ A 6 5 4
◇ 10 8 7 6
♣ 9 7 4

♠ 8 7 6 5
♡ K 3 2
◇ 9 5
♣ J 10 3 2

♠ A K J 10
♡ J 10 9 8
◇ A K Q 4
♣ 8

"Two top losers. What a contract!" hissed S.B.

"It's no disgrace to land in bad contracts," countered H.H. "It's allowing opponents to make them that's so humiliating. And let me tell you, Professor," went on the Hog, "that if you are never in a slam with a good five-card suit and a combined 32 count, you'll be a scrumptious loser. Yes, you'll lose even more than you should do. And finally," the Hog raised his voice and thumped the table, "allow me to inform you that I myself would win less than I deserve to do if I didn't, on occasion, land in impossible, in. . .er, indifferent contracts. Yes, I was South on this deal. Naturally, East didn't have the nerve to play low to the ♣ 6. He went up with the ten and returned a diamond. It happened to be a poor slam, I agree, but it was worth the same as a good one, 750 and the rubber points."

The Penguin drew a deep breath.

"Kindly don't interrupt, Peregrine," admonished H.H. "I was going to point out to all you purists and pedants that had North been dealt the ♡ K instead of the ♣ K, he would have bid the same way and 6 NT would have been unbeatable, played by North, and still an odds-on proposition with the lead coming from West. After all, he's not bound to lead a club, and half the time he would have the king himself."

The wild tufts of hair over the Secretary Bird's ears bristled with anger. The bloodless lips moved, but before a hiss could materialise, the Hideous Hog was in full spate again.

"There is more virtue," he declared, "in breaking one good contract than there be sin in fulfilling two bad ones." Then, dropping his voice, he turned to the Rabbit. "I wonder, R.R., if you would oblige me with another cheque."

There being no immediate response, the Hog seized the bill and jotted down two hands on the back.

Fourth Highest

"There you are," he went on, passing round the North–South hands.

Dealer South—Love All

```
        ♠ A Q 2
        ♡ K 7 4
        ◇ K J 10 4
        ♣ 6 5 4

        N
     W     E
        S

        ♠ J 9 7
        ♡ A 10 9
        ◇ A 8 6 5
        ♣ K J 3
```

South	North
1 NT	3 NT

"Who's who?" asked the Owl suspiciously.

"I won't tell you, just yet," replied the Hog. "I want you to play with an open mind. The lead is the ♠ 6. Let's say that you play low from dummy and that East's card is the ♠ 3. You win, and now need only eight more tricks. Go ahead."

Peregrine the Penguin was the first to speak: "If I find the ◇Q I'm home. If I misguess I shall have to rely on the clubs for my ninth trick."

"Since West is marked with length in spades," observed Oscar the Owl thoughtfully, "we should, I think, play East for the ◇Q, more especially since at this stage we would rather lose a trick to West than to East. We don't want a club through us for the moment, do we?"

"True," agreed the Penguin, "so let us play a diamond to the king, then the jack, finessing. . ."

"Don't bother," interrupted the Hog. "On the ◇K East drops the queen."

The Penguin shrugged his shoulders: "If, in addition to being short in spades, East has also a singleton diamond, he may be vulnerable to a squeeze in clubs and hearts."

"May we ask," chipped in the Secretary Bird, "whether we are playing for I.M.P.s, matchpoints or money?"

"Money," the Hog assured him; "and don't worry about overtricks. Just make the contract, if you can."

"If you insist," said P.P. coldly. "I come back to my hand with the ◇A and for my ninth trick I take the spade finesse. . . ."

"What you doubtless mean," corrected H.H., "is that you lead a spade, *intending* to finesse. On that spade, however, West throws a club, so it's hardly a finesse, is it?"

"Do you mean," exclaimed O.O., "that West led a singleton against 3 NT?"

"And that East, with six spades to the king, played the three?" asked P.P. incredulously.

"Papa, who was declarer, I may now tell you, was as astounded as you are," replied the Hog; "but that's how it was, and now the seemingly unbeatable contract became unmakable." The Hog filled in the other hands:

♠ A Q 2
♡ K 7 4
◇ K J 10 4
♣ 6 5 4

♠ 6   ♠ K 10 8 5 4 3
♡ Q 8 6 5   ♡ J 3 2
◇ 9 7 3 2   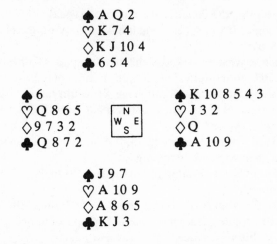   ◇ Q
♣ Q 8 7 2   ♣ A 10 9

♠ J 9 7
♡ A 10 9
◇ A 8 6 5
♣ K J 3

"What a ridiculous lead!" hissed the Secretary Bird.

"Positively surrealistic," said O.O. P.P. nodded in agreement.

"On the contrary," retorted the Hog, "it's a sound and sensible lead. Just reflect. West knows that East has five spades, if not six. Why? Because if North had four spades he would have surely used Stayman, and if South had five, he might not have opened 1 NT. So, you see, North–South can be expected to have seven spades at most between them, leaving a minimum of five for East. And since West has no high cards worth mentioning, he can place East with a certain entry, maybe with a couple of entries. Therefore he is quite right to open partner's suit, even though his card is a singleton."

"But what made East play the three? Third hand low. Is that a new convention, the Sicilian Defence or something?" asked the Toucan hopefully.

"A simple count-down from three to one," explained the Hog, "and I can now tell you that East was none other than your humble servant. I knew that the ♠ 6 couldn't be the lowest of three, for that would leave Papa with a singleton and he opened 1 NT. Having the ♠ 5 4 3 myself, I was in no doubt that the ♠ 6 was partner's lowest. From a doubleton he would have led the top, not the bottom card. So all my spades, apart from the king, were of the same value. But to exploit to the full the surprise element of a highly intelligent lead. . ."

"Who was West?" asked O.O. and P.P. in unison.

The Rabbit, his pink cheeks aglow, was fidgeting uncomfortably in his chair.

The Hog turned to him. "Allow me to introduce you," he said with a chuckle.

For a while this startling disclosure left everyone speechless. Oscar was the first to recover.

"And what," he asked, addressing R.R., "made you hit on this intell. . .on this, er, highly unusual lead?"

The Rabbit gurgled, but no coherent sound emerged from his throat and it was left to the Hog to provide the explanation.

"Much of the credit for this brilliant lead," he said, "should go to Charlie the Chimp, who was kibitzing. As usual, the Chimp was discussing the previous hand, or it may have been the one before, and R.R., again as usual, was caught up in the argument. His own lacklustre collection presenting little interest, he sorted out his cards carelessly, mixing up his spade with the clubs. Far from doing anything unusual," added H.H., "R.R. made the classical opening of the fourth-highest of his longest suit, only it so happened that his fourth-highest club was the ♠ 6."

"Unlucky to run up against this distribution, doubly unlucky to meet with this unexpectedly brilliant defence," observed the Owl. The Penguin concurred. The Secretary Bird hissed. The Rabbit's cheeks turned from crimson to magenta.

"Most unlucky," agreed the Hog, "but just as many a sound contract fails through bad luck, so many a bad one succeeds when fortune smiles. For my part, I like to make up on the swings what I lose on the roundabout—well, a bit more perhaps. And that is why, so long as I make them, I have no feelings of guilt about bad contracts."

Chapter 20
TO SIGNAL OR NOT TO SIGNAL?

Unable to heap any more oysters on his plate, the Hideous Hog conceded reluctantly the rest of the Colchesters. It was a good time to address him. With luck, if one did not pause too long for breath, an entire sentence might be completed without interruption.

Seizing the chance, Timothy the Toucan put the question: "Would you advise me to take up the Fisher Double?"

"Do you favour Michaels cue-bids?" asked the Rueful Rabbit.

"I strongly recommend both," replied H.H., nodding vigorously, as he applied the cayenne.

"Never heard of either whatsit," snorted Walter the Walrus. "What are they?"

"How d'y' expec' me to know?" snapped the Hog, despatching an oyster.

"If you don't know the conventions," protested the Toucan in injured tones, "how can you recommend them?"

"So emphatically, too," echoed the Rabbit indignantly.

Five Colchesters later, the Hog replied: "I recommend *all* conventions. It's elementary logic. I play twice as often against either of you as I do with you, though it doesn't seem like it, of course. It follows that for every three hundred, er, misfortunes that you perpet...that befall you, that is, I am one hundred to the good. And we play for money. So, you see, it's simply that one man's poison is another man's meat.

"As Lord Something so aptly said," went on H.H., "every convention creates confusion. All the conventions create total confusion. It is, therefore, in the public interest...well, in mine, anyway, that more people should play more conventions, and that is why I don't have to be familiar with MacFishers to commend it. Whatever it is, I am for it."

"But surely," objected the Rabbit, "some conventions are eminently useful. Take Blackwood, for example."

"Blackwood," replied H.H., "is not so much a convention as an emotional outlet. In theory, you check aces to keep out of slams when opponents have too many. In practice, aces are purely incidental. The 4 NT bid really means: 'I've a jolly good hand and though I can't think of what to say, I want to go places. Come with me.' Partner is delighted. Instead of having to think, he slips into a well fitting straitjacket and counts from none to one or two, or three at the outside. After all, when partner goes gay, he's unlikely to have a lot of aces himself."

The Rabbit drew in his breath and dipped an ear. He was probably on the point of saying something.

"On the contrary," retorted the Hideous Hog, "counting aces is a mere formality and can be dispensed with altogether. The operative phase of Blackwood is the hangover. You've heard about partner's aces and the ball is again in your court. You still don't know where to go and you are beginning to run out of distance, but you can't stop, for you're probably in 5 ◇, with a doubleton or something like that. So you bid a weak 5 NT with a shifty look and partner, rubbing salt in your wounds, tells you how many kings he has. Of course, you couldn't care less, because it wasn't aces or kings that you were curious about in the first place, but tricks and trumps and everyday things like that; but it's too late to go back and you can't go forward, because you don't know where you are. That's Blackwood for you."

"It's not the convention's fault if foolish people abuse it," protested the Walrus.

"Oh, but it is," insisted the Hog. "By their very nature, conventions invite abuse. In the case of Blackwood, the simplicity, which makes it so popular, is its gravest fault. How much easier to say '4 NT' than to make an intelligent cue-bid or to pave the way for one from partner."

"And yet," persisted the Rabbit, "I am sure that you use conventions yourself, in the play if not so much in the bidding. Now take signals. . . ."

"Of course I make use of signals," agreed the Hog, wrenching a leaf from an incoming artichoke. "I should hate to think what I would do without them. Fortunately the standard of signalling is high, so high that defenders can do it automatically, without having to think. For nine players out of ten these days signalling is not the means to an end, but an end in itself, a virtue; and like most virtues, it is its own reward."

A Helpful Signal

Hastily downing the Toucan's glass of Traminer, H.H. scribbled on a pad:

```
                    ♠ 8 5
                    ♡ A 7 5
                    ◇ A 3 2
                    ♣ 9 8 7 5 3

                    ┌─────┐
                    │  N  │
                    │W   E│
                    │  S  │
                    └─────┘

                    ♠ 7 6 3
                    ♡ K Q 3 2
                    ◇ K Q 10 4
                    ♣ A K
```

South	West	North	East
—	—	Pass	Pass
1 ◇	Pass	2 ♣	Pass
3 NT			

"There you are," said the Hog. "It's a hand I picked up a couple of days ago. West opened the deuce of spades, found East with A K J 9 and the defence took the first four tricks. I threw a heart and a club from dummy and a heart from my own hand. To the fifth trick West led a nondescript heart. Over to you my friends."

"Pity you let go that little heart," sighed R.R. "It might have come in handy. Now, I suppose, we must hope for a lucky diamond break."

"Or finesse against the jack," added the Toucan.

"It's a guess," said the Walrus, "though the odds. . ."

"The odds, my dear Walter, are heavily in favour of the *right* guess. If West has the jack to four of diamonds over you, there's no hope, so there's nothing to guess. If he hasn't. . ."

The Hog left the sentence unfinished and looked enquiringly at his audience. No one said anything, and as the silence grew louder, he continued: "You win the fifth trick in dummy with the ♡ A, and you proceed to cash the ace and king of clubs, then the king and queen of hearts. Having won five tricks, you go on to take the four diamonds, finessing or playing for a 3–3 break as the occasion demands."

"And *what* does the occasion demand?" asked the Walrus suspiciously. R.R. and T.T. nodded approvingly. It seemed a good question.

"That's where signalling is so useful," explained the Hog. "You may be sure that East and West will tell each other how many clubs they hold. Even if one of them has the sense to keep it to himself, the other one will blurt it out, for it isn't so easy to break oneself of these good habits. So you will either see them follow to the clubs in ascending order, or else one or the other, or both, will play high-low to show a 4–2 break."

"And then what?" persisted the Walrus.

"Then it's all over," replied H.H. "You will have a complete count on East. You saw him produce four spades. If he has three clubs and follows to three hearts, he must have three diamonds. If he shows out on the third heart, he must have four diamonds, so you play the king, the ace and finesse against the jack."

"But what if he plays high-low in clubs," persevered the Walrus, "how will you know whether he has two or four?"

"If he has four, he'll tell me," said the Hog, "for he'll have to throw a club, his third, on the third round of hearts, so he can't have a doubleton. Naturally," added H.H., noting that W.W. was about to speak, "East may follow to the hearts all the way, but if he has three hearts and also four clubs, we're sunk, for it will leave him with no more than a doubleton diamond.

"The point of the hand," went on the Hideous Hog, "is to play those two top clubs so as to get the signals going. If you take the hearts first and East shows out, he'll discard his lowest club and then, when the time comes, West won't signal either. You see," concluded the Hog, "how firmly I believe in signals."

This was the full deal:

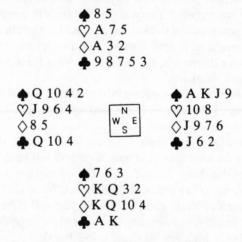

♠ 8 5
♥ A 7 5
♦ A 3 2
♣ 9 8 7 5 3

♠ Q 10 4 2
♥ J 9 6 4
♦ 8 5
♣ Q 10 4

♠ A K J 9
♥ 10 8
♦ J 9 7 6
♣ J 6 2

♠ 7 6 3
♥ K Q 3 2
♦ K Q 10 4
♣ A K

"Do you mean," asked T.T. incredulously, "that you don't signal in defence just because declarer may make greater use of the information than your partner?"

"It depends on what exactly you mean by signalling," replied the Hog, jotting down another hand. "Of course there are times when it's important to convey information. Now here's a case in point."

Biter Bit

♠ K 8 4
♡ K J 8 4
◇ K Q 10
♣ J 9 6

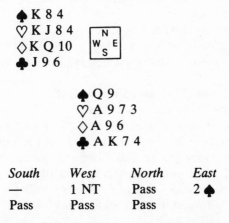

♠ Q 9
♡ A 9 7 3
◇ A 9 6
♣ A K 7 4

South	West	North	East
—	1 NT	Pass	2 ♠
Pass	Pass	Pass	

"South should pass 2 ♠ smoothly. He can see that he and West between them have 30 points, leaving 10 for the other two hands. Partner's share is 5, so it is clearly the time to defend. Pass, without registering doubt, and don't signal discomfort.

"The opening lead is the ♣ 10. You lead the two top clubs, then another. All follow, declarer winning with the queen in the closed hand. Next comes a spade to dummy's king and then another spade. Declarer's jack loses to your queen and the defence has now won three tricks. You need three more. Continue."

The Hog sat back to watch the flames leap over the *bécasse au fumet*.

"A low heart away from the ace," ventured R.R. "Declarer may misguess."

The Toucan bounced in agreement. "Yes, indeed," he said with feeling. "I am sure he'll misguess. All this talk about guessing right half the time, when it's a fifty-fifty chance. It's a gross exaggeration. . .never works out like that with me."

"Play the ♡ 9," suggested the Walrus: "a deceptive card, er. . ."

"Too deceptive," said the Hog. "If you persuaded declarer that you had no honour in hearts, it wouldn't matter which card he played from dummy. Half the time, no doubt, he would misguess. But I want him to misguess the other half of the time, too. I want to help him."

"How?" asked R.R. and T.T. in unison.

"By signalling," replied the Hog, good-humouredly sipping the Toucan's Corton, "by conveying information, as you put it just now."

"What information?" asked the Walrus.

"What signal?" echoed the Rabbit.

"The ◇ A, of course," said the Hog. "Declarer has seen you take three tricks with the ace and king of clubs and the queen of spades. That's nine points. Show him the ◇ A, signalling four more. Now, when you lead a heart, no declarer, that is no *ordinary* declarer, will place you with yet another ace. So he is most unlikely to play dummy's king, and you will have your misguess, or rather his."

"Oh, very clever, very clever indeed," enthused the Toucan. "You dazzled him with that ace and he played dummy's jack on the heart, and. . ."

"No, no," interrupted the Hideous Hog. "You've got it all wrong. I wasn't South. That was Papa's privilege. He made a well-judged pass over 2 ♠ and played ◇ A, and as I've just pointed out, no ordinary declarer would imagine that the 19 points he can't see are divided 17–2. Unfortunately for Papa he wasn't up against an ordinary declarer. *I* happened to be East, and I asked myself why Themistocles should so kindly display that ◇ A. Had he taken a sudden liking to me? Or was he signalling, imparting information, so to speak—not to his partner, who couldn't use it, but to me? A couple of seconds later I knew the answer. He showed me one red ace so that I shouldn't place him with the other. These were the hands:

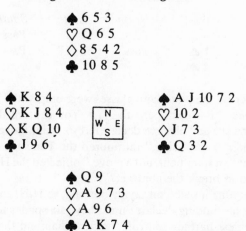

```
              ♠ 6 5 3
              ♡ Q 6 5
              ◇ 8 5 4 2
              ♣ 10 8 5

♠ K 8 4                      ♠ A J 10 7 2
♡ K J 8 4        N           ♡ 10 2
◇ K Q 10      W     E        ◇ J 7 3
♣ J 9 6          S           ♣ Q 3 2

              ♠ Q 9
              ♡ A 9 7 3
              ◇ A 9 6
              ♣ A K 7 4
```

"The moral of it," said the Hog, waving an accusing forefinger at the empty bottle, "is that the best signal will boomerang if you point it in the wrong direction. What was it that Browning said? Or was it Rupert Brooke? The best laid schemes o' East and West gang aft agley."

Psychic Signal

The Hog's voice trailed off as he sketched the familiar diagram. While he attended to the chocolate mousse, we studied the hands:

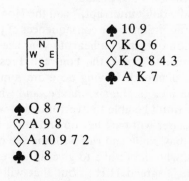

```
                    ♠ 10 9
                    ♡ K Q 6
         N          ◇ K Q 8 4 3
      W     E       ♣ A K 7
         S

                    ♠ Q 8 7
                    ♡ A 9 8
                    ◇ A 10 9 7 2
                    ♣ Q 8
```

West	North	East	South
—	Pass	1 ◇	Pass
1 ♠	Pass	2 NT	Pass
4 ♠			

When all the plates and glasses were empty, the Hideous Hog resumed: "Partner opens the ◇ J. You capture dummy's king with the ace and observe declarer's ◇6. Your move, Timothy."

"The ◇ 5 is missing," murmured the Toucan.

"That's a statement, not a move," objected the Hog. "What do you do to break the contract?"

Everyone insisted on saying nothing, so H.H. continued: "To justify his bidding declarer must have six spades to the A K, so that unless partner can ruff the next diamond there's precious little hope." There were acquiescent noises all round, and the Hog put the question:

"Which diamond, then, do you return for partner to ruff?"

"The ten," said the Toucan eagerly. "It's a suit signal, showing the ♡ A and calling for the higher-ranking of the other two suits for partner to play back."

Emptying his glass with a sigh of resignation, H.H. signalled to the sommelier for another bottle. "That's just what I've been telling you," he said sadly. "You signal because you find doing so pleasurable in itself. Why else should you ask partner to return a heart? What will you do if he complies?"

The Rabbit's lips parted.

"Kindly don't interrupt," said the Hog severely. "I was about to draw attention to the consequences of your suit signal. Partner will return obligingly a heart to your ace and you will need one more trick to break the contract. Presumably you will lead another diamond. Having no more himself, declarer will ruff with the jack or the six, maybe, and whatever it is your poor partner won't be able to overruff. That will expose your queen, and declarer will pick her up and make his contract."

"He may panic and ruff with the ace or king," suggested the Walrus, who didn't like to give up too easily.

"True," agreed H.H., "but that will make it all the more

certain that he will finesse against the queen, the only card that can break the contract."

"But how can I stop him?" expostulated the Rabbit.

"You should try," replied the Hog; "at least that's what I did. Instead of demanding a heart and signing my death warrant, I led the deuce of diamonds, requesting a club. Call it, if you like, a psychic suit signal. Partner duly returned a club, and declarer was put to a guess in trumps. Since North had ruffed once, four trumps only were out. He played for the drop. Unlucky."

The deal was:

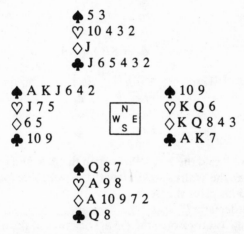

```
              ♠ 5 3
              ♡ 10 4 3 2
              ◇ J
              ♣ J 6 5 4 3 2

♠ A K J 6 4 2          N          ♠ 10 9
♡ J 7 5          W          E      ♡ K Q 6
◇ 6 5                 S            ◇ K Q 8 4 3
♣ 10 9                            ♣ A K 7

              ♠ Q 8 7
              ♡ A 9 8
              ◇ A 10 9 7 2
              ♣ Q 8
```

Walter the Walrus consulted his watch and shook his head. "It's later than I thought," he said with a sigh. "Even if I find a taxi, I shall be late for my appointment."

"What time is your appointment?" asked R.R., showing polite interest.

"A quarter of an hour ago," replied the Walrus, making for the door.

Petering with a Singleton

"That reminds me," broke in H.H. "An impeccable signaller, that Walrus." Another diagram was on the way:

Dealer North—Love All
W.W.

C.C.   **Papa**
♠ Q 6 2
♡ A J 3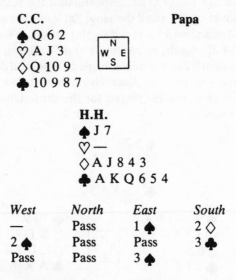
♢ Q 10 9
♣ 10 9 8 7

H.H.
♠ J 7
♡ —
♢ A J 8 4 3
♣ A K Q 6 5 4

West	North	East	South
—	Pass	1 ♠	2 ♢
2 ♠	Pass	Pass	3 ♣
Pass	Pass	3 ♠	

"There," said the Hog. "You open the ♣ K and partner, none other than the Walrus, greets it with the jack. You follow with the ♢ A and he plays the deuce."

"And declarer?" asked the Toucan.

"The ♣ 3 at trick one, the ♢ 5 at trick two. Make of it what you will, bearing in mind, of course, that you need three more tricks to break the contract."

"How about underleading your top clubs, hoping that partner will ruff?" suggested the Rabbit. "You would play the highest of your low clubs, an unmistakable suit preference signal, so. . ."

"So you would make four tricks." The Hog finished the sentence for him. "Not enough."

"And you made five?" asked R.R.

"No." The Hog was chortling. "I made six, and there was nothing that poor Papa, who happened to be declarer, could do about it."

"Come, come," he went on, noting the puzzled looks around him. "You've had your signals. What do you lead at trick three?"

The Toucan bounced. The Rabbit gurgled. Neither spoke.

"Why, the ◇ J, of course," said H.H. "What you called just now an unmistakable suit preference signal."

"But Walrus signalled in clubs," objected T.T. "He played the jack and, in diamonds, the deuce."

"It couldn't have been a psychic signal, I suppose," ventured the Rabbit, "like yours on that other hand?"

The Hog looked at him pityingly. Turning to the Toucan, he explained: "Think of the bidding. I called diamonds first, then clubs, and the Walrus had passed, giving clubs preference. Yet here he was signalling a doubleton. What, then, was his deuce of diamonds? Since it couldn't be the lowest of three—or he would have shown a preference for diamonds—it had to be a singleton.

"It only remained for me to give him a ruff, calling for a heart back, another diamond ruff, a second heart ruff and we had six tricks, one more than we needed—and all because of simple signals.

"More often than you think," concluded the Hog with a chuckle, "higher mathematics in bridge consist in counting correctly up to two—and drawing the right inference, of course."

Chapter 21

STRAINED RELATIONS

Relations between the Hog and Papa, never of the best, have been exacerbated recently by two unfortunate incidents. It all began, however, with a third one, but for which the others might not have happened.

This is how it all started.

We were chatting in the Griffins bar before lunch one day, looking at a hand on which Papa had gone down the previous night in the weekly duplicate at the Unicorn.

He was just saying: "I gave myself the only chance, but there was no play for it", when the Hog walked over, glass in hand, to join us. Recognising the hand and pretending not to have heard Papa, he began in his most patronising manner.

"Ah, yes, I had it in our first set of boards and gave myself a shade above average:

Dealer East—Game All

```
              ♠ Q 7 5 4
              ♡ Q J 10 9 8
              ◇ K 10
              ♣ K 6
♠ 10 9 8                      ♠ K J 6
♡ 6 4 3 2         N          ♡ K 7 5
◇ 5            W     E        ◇ J 6
♣ J 5 4 3 2       S          ♣ A Q 10 8 7
              ♠ A 3 2
              ♡ A
              ◇ A Q 9 8 7 4 3 2
              ♣ 9
```

West	North	East	South
—	—	1 ♣	2 ♣
Pass	3 ♣	Pass	3 ◇
Pass	3 ♡	Pass	4 ◇
Pass	5 ◇		

"That was our sequence, but most pairs, I suppose, reached 5◇; though 3 NT played by North is a lot better, of course, if you can get there. Against that, some of the weaker brethren may have found a way of going down in 5 ◇. After all," he added with a sly look at the Greek from the corner of his eye, "there's one born every minute, they say. So, on balance. . ."

"You know perfectly well," broke in Papa, "that against proper defence 5 ◇is unmakable. No doubt, some crazy East, one of your weaker brethren, thoughtlessly discarded a spade. . . ."

"A spade?" repeated H.H., as if he had never heard of the suit. "But didn't you get a club lead to East's queen, then the ace?"

"Naturally," replied the Greek, "and I gave myself the one and only chance, a doubleton ♠ K. But it was not to be, and though I reeled off my trumps, they kept the right cards. No doubt you performed some masterstroke and talked them out of it."

"I didn't have to perform anything. Just a baby play."

"What did you do at trick three, after ruffing the ♣ A?" asked Papa.

"At trick three, I wasn't on play," replied the Hog smugly and, seeing the blank looks around him, he proceeded to explain: "On the ♣ A I quickly jettisoned the ♡ A. After that, so long as the trumps were not 3–0, I could claim."

Papa looked daggers at him, but said nothing.

"You don't see it?" went on H.H. "Oh, very well, I'll dot the 'is'. On his opening bid East is pretty well marked with the kings in both majors, so what can he do when I leave him on play, after unblocking the hearts, of course?

"If he leads away from either king he surrenders at once. Another club, presenting me with a ruff and discard, is no better.

So he leads a trump, but that creates a second entry to dummy and allows a ruffing finesse in hearts."

The Hog raised his glass. "To your good health, Papa. But perhaps you are not satisfied, and would like to break the contract. Any suggestions?"

"I admit that I played too quickly last night, but that doesn't excuse your odious gloating. And anyway," added the Greek with a contemptuous smile, "since you have proved that the contract is unbeatable, it wasn't so very clever of you to make it, was it?"

Beating the Unbeatable

"What!" cried the Hog. "You think that this contract, unmakable a couple of minutes ago, is now unbeatable?"

An angry spluttering noise was the Greek's only response. Just in case he found the answer, however, H.H. proceeded to give it himself.

"All East has to do," explained the Hog in the manner of a teacher addressing a kindergarten class, "is not to play the ♣ A. At trick two he switches to a trump, removing one of dummy's possible entries while the hearts are still blocked. You see, Papa," taunted the Hog, "you were right all the time, though you didn't know it." And, laughing loudly, he walked away.

Calm before the Storm

It was unfortunate that the same day, while Papa's wounds were still raw, he cut the Hog in a rubber against the Secretary Bird and the Rueful Rabbit.

As usual, kibitzers gathered quickly when word went round that the two natural enemies were facing each other in unnatural alliance. No one wanted to miss a single word of abuse.

"Usual side bet, Papa?" asked S.B., the Emeritus Professor of Bio-Sophistry.

"No, we'll give it a miss this time," replied the Greek, looking H.H. firmly in the eye. "I don't like to bet unless I play myself, and I am hardly likely to do much of that this rubber."

This was the first deal:

Papa
♠ A 7 6
♡ 6 5 4 3 2
◇ A J 6
♣ A 7

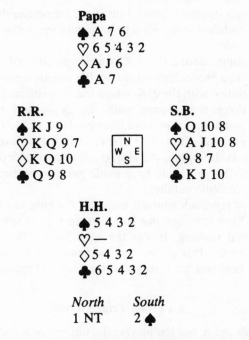

R.R.
♠ K J 9
♡ K Q 9 7
◇ K Q 10
♣ Q 9 8

S.B.
♠ Q 10 8
♡ A J 10 8
◇ 9 8 7
♣ K J 10

H.H.
♠ 5 4 3 2
♡ —
◇ 5 4 3 2
♣ 6 5 4 3 2

North	South
1 NT	2 ♠

The auction, and more especially the Hog's call of 2 ♠, may appear somewhat unorthodox. But as H.H. later told an enquiring kibitzer, it was a routine sequence to which there could be no conceivable alternative.

"Any mathematician will tell you," explained the Hog, "that partner's 13-point notrump, added to my zero, leaves opponents with some 27 points. Inevitably, the 1 NT will be doubled and the resulting penalty can hardly be less than 700. A weakness take-out is, therefore, imperative, and since 2 ♣ would be interpreted as Stayman, the choice lies between 2 ◇ and 2 ♠. The latter is preferable on account of its pre-emptive value, and also because opponents are less likely to double a bid which, if made, will give the other side a game.

"Finally," concluded H.H., "though my hand is not rich in

tenaces, it is always an advantage that the opening lead should run up to the stronger player."

The Hog's optimism proved justified, for no one doubled his 2 ♠. His confident tone, allied to his reputation, sufficed to deter the other side.

The Rabbit opened the ◇ K, which was allowed to win. No switch looked particularly attractive, but a heart seemed safe and R.R. continued with the ♡ K, which the Hog ruffed. Crossing to dummy three times, once with the ♣ A and twice with diamonds—taking the marked finesse—H.H. ruffed three more hearts in his hand. That came to seven tricks. Pointing to the ace of trumps as the eighth, the Hog graciously conceded the rest.

"I think that we could have made game in notrumps," ventured the Rabbit ruefully.

"Do not reproach yourself unduly," the Hog reassured him. "As you have just seen, we had a cheap save in spades."

Papa said nothing. It was the calm before the storm, the overture to the first of the two incidents which have brought relations between the Greek and the Hog to breaking point.

A Certain Trump Trick

Papa dealt again, but the players did not notice it and the kibitzers did not seem to mind. At 60 up, the Greek had no hesitation in opening the bidding with 1 ♣. Tactically, with a part-score, substandard openings are sound enough. If partner has the cards, it makes little difference. But if opponents hold the balance of power, each in turn is inclined to suspect the other of stretching to save game, with the result that they sometimes fail to reach an easy game themselves:

Papa
♠ 7 5 4
♡ 4 3
♢ K J 10
♣ A K 4 3 2

R.R.
♠ 10 9 8
♡ 8 7 6 5 2
♢ 2
♣ J 7 6 5

```
  N
W   E
  S
```

S.B.
♠ K J
♡ K J 9
♢ 9 8 6 5 4 3
♠ Q 10

H.H.
♠ A Q 6 3 2
♡ A Q 10
♢ A Q 7
♣ 9 8

West	North	East	South
—	1 ♣	1 ♢	2 ♠
Pass	3 ♣	Pass	3 ♢
Pass	3 ♠	Pass	4 NT
Pass	5 ♢	Pass	5 NT
Pass	6 ♣	Pass	7 ♢!

The first three rounds of bidding were uneventful. Over Papa's 1 ♣, S.B. intervened with 1 ♢ and the Hog forced with 2 ♠. Opponents took no further part in the bidding, and the Greek repeated his clubs. The Hog now bid the enemy suit, 3 ♢, and Papa signed off quietly in 3 ♠. Beginning to feel a little uncomfortable, he showed his ace over 4 NT, but when H.H. went on to 5 NT, Papa felt that he had done enough. Suppressing the existence of his two kings, the Greek's 6 ♣ bid was intended to banish for ever all thoughts of a grand slam.

On the Hog, the 6 ♣ bid had precisely the opposite effect. Unable to visualise Papa's hand without a king in it, he assumed that the Greek was showing all four. Just as 5 ♣ over 4 NT promises four aces or none, so an extension of the same principle should apply to kings. By this time there was no doubt in the Hog's mind that the North–South hands would yield thirteen tricks. But what in? If Papa's clubs were solid, the hand should be played in notrumps. If not, 7 ♠ might prove the better contract. Only Papa could know the answer, and to put the picture clearly before him the Hog produced a master bid: 7 ◇, leaving it to Themistocles Papadopoulos to deliver the verdict at the seven level.

Papa blinked. He blinked again. Then his eyes narrowed as in his feverish imagination he detected a Machiavellian design behind the Hog's bidding sequence. Whatever he did, the Hog, as always, would play the hand. And if anything went wrong—and it could hardly be otherwise—Papa would be held responsible on account of his substandard opening. It was a bitter thought, but he was forced to admit that, once again, the Hideous Hog had endplayed him in the bidding. And then, suddenly, through black despair flashed the vision of escape, a dazzling exit-bid to which H.H. would have no answer. He would bid neither 7 ♠ nor 7 NT. He would simply pass 7 ◇! Since he was bound to be abused anyway, at least he would have the satisfaction of deserving it—and of teaching that Hog a salutary lesson in the process.

The Secretary Bird passed gleefully, and a gasp went up from the serried ranks of kibitzers. Not one of them had yet seen a grand slam played in a cue-bid.

"I must say!" Walter the Walrus could be heard whispering across the room. "Fancy not doubling with ten and a half points, and a certain trump trick, too."

S.B. hissed disdainfully. The gentle smirk, the superior smile on his thin, bloodless lips, told the world that he knew when he was on to a good thing, and he had no intention of painting the beautiful lily.

The Rabbit opened the ♡ 8 and the Hog, still hurling imprecations at Papa, won the trick with the ten. Not pausing a second in his tirade, he crossed to dummy with a club and took the marked finesse in hearts. After cashing the ace and throwing a spade from dummy, he went back with his second club and finessed against the ♠ K. Scoring his seventh trick with the ♠ A, the Hog sat back. Without another word of abuse, he proceeded to reel off six more tricks on a crossruff. Three times, when spades were led from the closed hand and ruffed in dummy, the Emeritus Professor underruffed. Three times, when clubs were led from dummy, the Hog overruffed the Professor.

"You see how wise our friend was not to double," said the Hog, chuckling, to the Walrus. "A certain trump trick does not always defeat a grand slam, you know—not when I am at the wheel, anyway."

The Hog, flushed with success, was now in his most insufferable mood. With a pitying look he said to the Greek: "Never mind, Themistocles, you meant well, I am sure, and maybe my bidding was a bit too advanced for you. Still we reached the only makable grand slam on the cards, so I. . .er, we did not do so badly."

Papa gnashed his teeth. Never had he enjoyed making a grand slam as much as he regretted not losing this one.

A Fateful Board

The critical match between the Griffins and the Dinosaurs for the Salamander Cup took place the very next day. Under the rules of this competition every player in the team must, in turn, partner every other player.

In view of the tension between Papa and the Hog, Oscar, our non-playing captain, kept them apart until the last set of boards. By then he hoped that a healthy lead would stop either of these 'individualists', as he called them, from trying to win the match single-handed.

Things, however, did not go well for the Griffins, and after twenty boards they were 1,130 down.

I watched the last part of the match in the room where Colin the Corgi and the Secretary Bird opposed the Dinosaurs' star pair, Lord Mortsbury, President of International Morticians Inc., and his export manager, Jocelyn Joybell.

The Griffins began badly, missing a vulnerable game which

they played in the wrong contract. Otherwise the first nine hands were uneventful. This was the last board of the match:

Dealer North—Game All

J.J.
♠ Q 7 5
♡ J 10
♢ Q J 10 9 8 7 6
♣ 10

C.C.　　　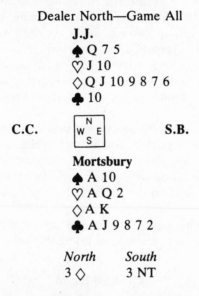　　　**S.B.**

Mortsbury
♠ A 10
♡ A Q 2
♢ A K
♣ A J 9 8 7 2

North	South
3 ♢	3 NT

Colin led the ♠ 6. Mortsbury inserted dummy's ♠ 7 and won the Professor's ♠ 8 with the ♠ 10 in his hand.

Next he cashed the ♢ A K and continued hopefully with the ♡ Q. This, however, was allowed to hold, and after much puffing and blowing he ended up two down.

"Bad luck," said J.J.

"Yes, wasn't it?" echoed C.C., seizing the chance for a friendly jeer. "How much luckier it would have been had declarer won the first trick with the ♠ A, cashed the ♢ A K and then exited with the ♠ 10 to my king. I couldn't have returned a spade or a heart, without giving access to the diamonds, and a club switch would have been just as fatal."

"Your partner might have had the ♠ K," objected J.J., coming gallantly to his chief's defence.

"Not really. The rule of eleven and all that," rejoined the Corgi breezily. "If my six was the fourth highest, and there could be no reason for a false lead, five higher cards were out. Four of them were on view, the A 10 in the closed hand and the Q 7 in dummy. My partner's 8 was the fifth. So I had to have the king. Besides," added C.C. sweetly, "there was no other way of being lucky, was there?"

"They're waiting for the board," said Oscar, looking in from the other room. As I took it across, he whispered to me: "We are 1610 down."

Papa Loses his Temper

With the result a foregone conclusion, I sat down to watch with a sense of anticlimax, relieved only by the malevolent looks exchanged between Papa and the Hog.

Like J.J., the Hog opened 3 ◇ and like Mortsbury, the Greek bid 3 NT. Thereafter, however, events followed a very different course. This was the sequence:

West	North	East	South
—	3 ◇	Pass	3 NT
Pass	4 ◇	Pass	5 ♣
Dble	5 ◇	Pass	?

The Greek drew in his breath. On this, the last board of an ill-fated match, that odious Hog was still going to have his way. Regardless of the cards, openly contemptuous of his partner, he was determined to play the hand. It was the last straw, and it broke the camel's back.

With beads of perspiration rolling down his forehead, his hand shaking, his voice two full octaves higher than usual, he announced: "I will now save two rounds of bidding: 7 ◇!"

There was stunned silence. Every Griffin present knew that Papa had been goaded beyond endurance by the Hog's endless jeers and jibes and studied insults. Worse still, Papa had come off second-best in every acrimonious encounter. These were mitigating circumstances, but they didn't excuse a vicious, bad-tempered outburst and the Griffins were deeply shocked.

Papa knew it, and there and then he began to formulate a letter of resignation to the club Secretary. He had already reached 'Dear Sir' when the ♣ 4 was placed on the table.

Sensing what had happened, even though they didn't know the background, the Dinosaurs were too sporting to double. After the double of 5 ♣, however, the opening lead was automatic.

This was the deal in full:

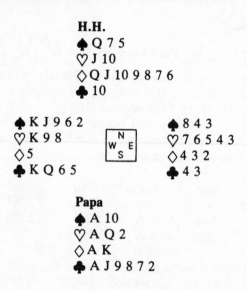

H.H.
♠ Q 7 5
♡ J 10
◇ Q J 10 9 8 7 6
♣ 10

♠ K J 9 6 2
♡ K 9 8
◇ 5
♣ K Q 6 5

♠ 8 4 3
♡ 7 6 5 4 3
◇ 4 3 2
♣ 4 3

Papa
♠ A 10
♡ A Q 2
◇ A K
♣ A J 9 8 7 2

H.H. Wins the Match

The Hog went up with dummy's ace and ruffed a club. Returning to dummy with the ◇ A, he ruffed another club. Back with the ◇ K, he ruffed a third club, setting up two clubs in dummy. There was still a trump out, so he drew it, leaving this position:

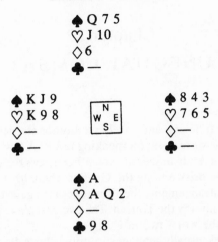

```
        ♠ Q 7 5
        ♡ J 10
        ◇ 6
        ♣ —

♠ K J 9            ♠ 8 4 3
♡ K 9 8    N       ♡ 7 6 5
◇ —      W   E     ◇ —
♣ —        S       ♣ —

        ♠ A
        ♡ A Q 2
        ◇ —
        ♣ 9 8
```

Crossing to the ♡ A, he cashed the clubs. On the first one West could let go a spade, but the second one was a killer. If he parted with a heart, the Hog would do likewise. Then he would ruff a heart, setting up the queen, and get back to it with the ♠ A. If West threw a spade, the ♠ Q would be the Hog's thirteenth trick.

West surrendered.

The Hog had brought off the grand slam on a trump squeeze, and so had won the match for the Griffins.

With what was doubtless intended as an amiable smile, he addressed the Dinosaurs. "You must forgive Mr Papadopoulos," he began. "He is, at times, a little temperamental, but when the occasion calls for it, he can be brilliant, as you have just seen. Knowing that his play had not been too, er, felicitous on the other boards, he realised that we needed nothing less than a grand slam on this one. Observe how careful he was to avoid the risk of steering the contract into the wrong hand. That bold jump to 7 ◇, a trifle unusual, perhaps, was indeed inspired. Well done, Papa, and thank you, gentlemen, for a most enjoyable game."

Just as he was about to word the first paragraph, Papa decided to tear up his letter of resignation.

Chapter 22

UNEQUAL COMBAT

Time is a great healer, and barely six months elapsed before the Hog and Papa were again on speaking terms. A few weeks more and they were ready to jeer at each other across the green baize.

Betting was brisk among the Griffins when, for the first time since their estrangement, they cut together against the Rueful Rabbit and Timothy the Toucan. The two best players in the club were facing the worst two in Europe.

"The Greek usually manages to outwit himself, and he may outwit the Hog too," murmured Colin the Corgi. The oyster season had started, and having taken 100–6 in Whitstables against the Rabbit, he was looking on the bright side of things.

The rubber was about to start when M. Merle announced that the lobster soufflé was ready and would be ruined if we kept it waiting As we adjourned for dinner I could hear the Rabbit stiffening the Toucan's quivering sinews.

"Keep calm, Timothy," he was saying, "just concentrate on holding good cards. You've read that book I gave you on the latest conventions? Good. Well, we'll give them everything: Landy, Astro, Ripstra, Gerber, negative doubles. . . ."

"Blackwood?" asked the Toucan eagerly.

"Of course," the Rabbit assured him, "and Roman Blackwood and Flint, Fisher, Fishbein, San Francisco, Texas. . ."

"I haven't quite got to the 'Ts'," protested the Toucan but a champagne cork drowned his voice.

Pre-Empting on a Doubleton

Tension ran high as first one side, then the other, collected a part-score. The Hog and Papa were 30 up when this hand came up:

Papa
♠ J 10 7 6
♡ A 6 5 4 3
◇ 6 4
♣ 5 4.

R.R.
♠ A Q 5 2
♡ K Q J 10
◇ J 10 8
♣ J 9

T.T.
♠ K 4 3
♡ 8 7
◇ 9 7 5 3
♣ K Q 10 7

```
        N
     W     E
        S
```

H.H.
♠ 9 8
♡ 9 2
◇ A K Q 2
♣ A 8 6 3 2

South	West	North	East
1 NT	Pass	2 ♣	Pass
2 ♠	2 NT	Pass	3 ♣
Dble	Pass	3 ♠	Pass
Pass	Dble		

The Toucan, who had been trying to master too many conventions at once, enquired whether Papa's 2 ♣ was the Little Major. The Hog assured him that it was Stayman and Papa, in turn, explained that the Hog's response showed four spades. "Could even be five," he added. "It is quite the fashion nowadays to open a notrump with a weak five-card major."

H.H. nodded approvingly. He had every intention of playing like a man with five trumps.

The Rabbit's ♡ K held the first trick, the Toucan petering with the eight and H.H. dropping the nine. The ♡ Q followed, and the goddess of justice stumbled and seemed to slip. As the scales fell from her hands, the Hideous Hog went up with dummy's ace, ruffed a heart in his hand, cashed his three top diamonds, throwing a club from dummy, and continued with the ace of clubs. That came to six tricks. A club ruff in dummy and another heart ruffed in the closed hand brought the total to eight. Now a club towards the table made certain of the contract. Whether or not the Rabbit ruffed high, dummy would have a trump trick.

"Simple dummy reversal," declared H.H. with a friendly leer at Papa.

"Perhaps I should have ruffed that heart with my king," murmured the Toucan apologetically. "But somehow it didn't seem natural."

"Did you have the nerve to advertise four spades with a wretched doubleton?" asked the Greek, narrowing his eyes.

"With part-scores about, one has to depart from orthodoxy," retorted the Hog. "My first concern was to shut them out." And in a loud aside to Oscar he added: "One doesn't like to pre-empt on a two-card suit, but I could hardly let him massacre the hand in hearts or something, could I? Besides, what other game contract did we have?"

"In the other room," chipped in the Corgi with a grin, "they also made game—2 NT played the other way."

"He laughs best who laughs last," muttered Papa softly, picking up the next hand.

Endplay before Trick One

Since Papa became declarer, he is shown as sitting South:

H.H.
♠ A K Q J
♡ J 10 9 8 7
♢ 5 2
♣ 4 2

T.T.

```
  N
W   E
  S
```

R.R.

Papa
♠ 10
♡ A K Q
♢ A Q 8 7 6
♣ A Q 5 3

South	West	North	East
2 ♢	Pass	2 ♡	Pass
3 ♢	Pass	3 ♠	Pass
3 NT	Pass	4 NT	Pass
6 NT	Dble	Pass	Pass
Redble			

Oscar the Owl viewed the auction with obvious distaste. "Surely," he told the Greek later, "you should have supported the hearts at some stage."

"And let him play the hand?" asked Papa incredulously.

"Well then," persisted Oscar, "you should have shown your clubs. H.H. might have had a perfect fit."

"He would never have admitted it," retorted the Greek; "and had I given him the chance, he would have got the notrumps in first. I had to think ahead. The theory of anticipation, you know."

That anyone so meek and humble as the Toucan should double a slam freely bid by his betters came as a shock to the kibitzers. To show his lack of confidence in his partner, H.H. carefully refrained from redoubling and Papa had to perform this menial task himself.

It was some time before the Toucan could be prevailed upon to lead, but eventually he found the ♠ 8.

To a lesser player the lead might have proved embarrassing. Papa took it in his stride. He played out dummy's four top spades, discarding his ace, king and queen of hearts. Then he led out dummy's hearts, watching the discards. Both defenders followed all the way to the spades, but the Toucan, having no hearts, threw four clubs and a diamond. Papa's last four cards were the ◇ A Q and the ♣ A Q.

"I rather think you had the temerity to double me," he said in icy tones to the Toucan, who had been shrinking visibly trick by trick. "Very rash, my friend," went on the Greek. "Without your help I would now have to take a finesse, and since your double marks you with the K x in both minors, I would, alas, lose it. You would return the same suit and I should have to concede a trick to your other king. Now, however," continued Papa, "you are at my mercy, for your thoughtless double has given the game away. Yes, you endplayed yourself before leading the first card."

Appearing not to notice the Hog, who was oozing hatred from every pore, Papa pursued his monologue as he led a diamond from dummy: "So our friend R.R. follows with the nine. Good. I go up with my ace and continue with the queen, putting Timothy in with the king. Let him now lead a club into my major tenace. Like this! So!" On the ◇ Q the Toucan dropped the jack. The Rabbit grasped the trick with his king and made another with the ten, for the cards had been dealt like this:

H.H.
♠ A K Q J
♡ J 10 9 8 7
♢ 5 2
♣ 4 2

T.T.
♠ 8 7 6 5
♡ —
♢ J 4 3
♣ J 10 9 8 7 6

```
      N
   W     E
      S
```

R.R.
♠ 9 4 3 2
♡ 6 5 4 3 2
♢ K 10 9
♣ K

Papa
♠ 10
♡ A K Q
♢ A Q 8 7 6
♣ A Q 5 3

There was a deathly silence broken only by the gnashing of the Hog's teeth.

"What on earth made you double, Timothy?" asked Oscar the Owl.

"It was the, er, Lightner double," replied the Toucan almost inaudibly. "I had been reading about it. Having no hearts, you see. . ."

"But it was your own lead," broke in a kibitzer.

"And why should you want a heart lead, anyway, in a notrump contract?" asked another.

"One can't always think of everything," countered the Rueful Rabbit, springing to his partner's defence. "Perhaps we have been trying to work in too many conventions. . . ."

"In the other room. . ." began Colin the Corgi.

"Why don't you go and stay there?" cried Papa and H.H. in unison. For the first time that evening they saw eye to eye.

Chapter 23

DELUSIONS OF GRANDEUR

"Let's go back to the Griffins for a friendly rubber," suggested the Rabbit.

"Couldn't start the New Year better," agreed the Toucan enthusiastically.

The Hideous Hog looked disdainfully at the Secretary Bird. S.B. viewed H.H. with unconcealed distaste.

"Come, come, the New Year spirit," pleaded Timothy the Toucan. His articulation, I thought, was a little slurred, but he exuded bonhomie from every pore.

It had been a rousing New Year party at the Bunny Club, with the Rabbit, an honorary life member, setting a splendid example of conviviality. The Emeritus Professor of Bio-Sophistry objected that the hour was late. Having lost the toss, he had to drive the rest of us home and his celebrations had been confined to six bitter lemons, a tomato juice and two glasses of Champagne, one of which the Hog had swallowed in error.

Eventually, S.B. gave way. "All right," he agreed grudgingly, "I'll play for a while, but no new rubbers after five o'clock."

This was the first hand:

S.B.
♠ 8 7 6 5
♡ 6 5 4 3
◇ A 10 3
♣ A 3

R.R.
♠ 4
♡ —
◇ Q 8 7 6 5 4
♣ Q J 10 9 8 7

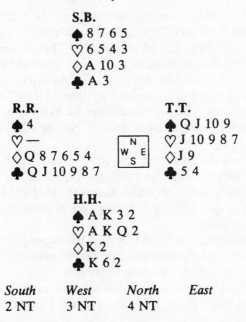

T.T.
♠ Q J 10 9
♡ J 10 9 8 7
◇ J 9
♣ 5 4

H.H.
♠ A K 3 2
♡ A K Q 2
◇ K 2
♣ K 6 2

South	West	North	East
2 NT	3 NT	4 NT	

The Hideous Hog greeted the New Year by dealing himself a full-blooded 2 NT opening, and an *avant-garde* bidding sequence followed.

The Rabbit boldly invoked the Unusual Notrump procedure in an unusual situation, only to be countered by S.B.'s 4 NT, which shut out all competition.

A Convivial Defence

The Rabbit opened the ♣ Q. Winning in dummy, the Hog led a spade, allowing the Toucan's nine to hold the trick. A club came back and, after a momentary pause, the Hog went up with his king. Next he played the ♠ A and when the Rabbit threw a diamond, he tested the hearts. Again R.R. showed out, and the whole picture came into view. Even so, playing double dummy, only nine tricks were available. Was there any way of conjuring up one more?

While the Hog examined his prospects, the Rabbit, blissfully tipsy, focused a smile on each of us in turn. "I like you," he announced. "I like you all very much." Then, solemnly, he laid out his cards face downwards in the order in which he expected to play them. It was all so simple. He had thrown one diamond on the second round of spades and another on the ♡ A. He would retain the queen and two more diamonds to the end, and cling on to as many winning clubs as possible. No one could talk him out of it.

Matching the Hog for speed, R.R. turned over his cards, one by one, flicking them neatly to the centre of the table. After cashing the ♠ K and two more hearts, the Hog was left with ♠ 2 ♡ 2 ◇ K 2 ♣ 2. Exiting with the deuce of clubs, he now put the Rabbit on play.

"Same again," declared R.R. jauntily, turning up the ♣ J. But though he carefully scrutinised his four remaining cards, not one of them was a club. All were diamonds.

"I seem to have thrown a winner inadvertently," he said in consternation. "Sorry, Timothy. I mean, I didn't mean. . .I. . . er. . ."

"Take back your last discard or the one before, if you like," offered the Hog magnanimously. "Can't take advantage of a slip like that on a festive evening. All through *joie de vivre*, too." H.H. was insistent, but the Rabbit would have none of it. With a subdued, apologetic hiccup he led a diamond—and the suicide squeeze, so carefully planned by the Hog, died before it could take shape.

Once again the Rabbit's guardian angel, powerfully assisted by Bacchus, had saved him from himself. Without their intervention the Rabbit would have had a second club in place of a fourth diamond in the five-card end position, which would have been:

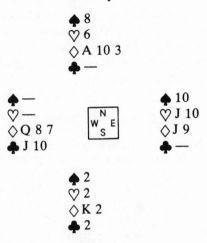

♠ 8
♡ 6
◇ A 10 3
♣ —

♠ —
♡ —
◇ Q 8 7
♣ J 10

♠ 10
♡ J 10
◇ J 9
♣ —

♠ 2
♡ 2
◇ K 2
♣ 2

The Toucan had a heart to throw on the ♣ J, but when R.R. announced 'same again', he could already feel the sword of Damocles tickling his Adam's apple. For if he parted with a spade or a heart, the Hog, discarding after him, would be presented with a trick in that suit. If he let go a diamond, the jack would drop on the king and the Hog would score his tenth trick by taking the marked finesse against the queen. From this horrible trilemma the Toucan was saved by the Rabbit's careless discard of a winner.

"It looks to me," observed Colin the Corgi, who had joined the ranks of kibitzers, "that R.R. plays much better when he doesn't see the face of the cards. Maybe, as a New Year resolution, he might like to adopt this style. . . ."

But the Rueful Rabbit wasn't listening. He was gazing apprehensively at the Toucan, for there was an unmistakable roll in his movements as he bounced uncertainly in his chair, the long crimson nose outlined against the midnight blue of his dinner jacket. T.T. had greeted the New Year with much enthusiasm, and was now showing signs of strain. He would have been more at ease, one suspected, had the room been properly equipped with stabilisers.

Taking in the situation at a glance, the Rabbit decided to take charge and protect his disabled partner, just as he himself had been so often protected by the Hideous Hog. Even when he had taken no stimulant beyond a teaspoonful of Eno's, H.H. would say 'Sober but incapable', and he would invariably take control. The Rabbit resolved to do likewise.

A Defence Too Perfect

To steady the room a bit, he changed places with T.T., seating him by the open window. Soon, this hand came along:

```
                T.T.
                ♠ 8 3 2
                ♡ Q 4 2
                ◇ A Q J 10 9
                ♣ Q 8

    H.H.                        S.B.
                                ♠ K J 10
            N                   ♡ 10 8 7
        W       E               ◇ K 8 7 6
            S                   ♣ 7 5 4

                R.R.
```

South	West	North	East
1 NT	Pass	2 NT	Pass
3 NT			

The Hog opened the ♠ 6 and the Emeritus Professor crossed his long legs, the better to study the situation. On the rule of eleven declarer had one card only higher than the six. If it were the ace or alternatively the nine or seven, it wouldn't matter which card S.B. played. But if it were the queen, especially the doubleton queen, the suit would be blocked. The king would win the first trick, the queen would fall to the ace and S.B. would be back to play with the ten. No doubt H.H had an entry somewhere, but before S.B. could find it, the Rabbit might set up dummy's diamonds and rattle off nine tricks. Certain of regaining the lead in time with the ◇K, the Secretary Bird made the farsighted play of the ♠ 10.

Winning with the ♠ A, R.R. crossed to dummy with the ◇A and led the ♣ Q, following with the deuce from the closed hand. The Hog took the trick with the king and looked around. Sparks flew from the wild tufts of hair over S.B.'s ears as he willed his partner to press on with spades. The Hog appeared to be in some doubt. To see what was troubling him, I walked round the table to look at the other hands.

This was the deal:

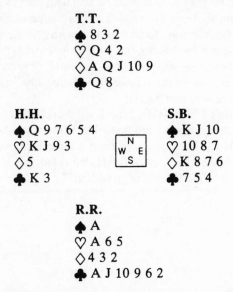

T.T.
♠ 8 3 2
♡ Q 4 2
◇ A Q J 10 9
♣ Q 8

H.H.
♠ Q 9 7 6 5 4
♡ K J 9 3
◇ 5
♣ K 3

S.B.
♠ K J 10
♡ 10 8 7
◇ K 8 7 6
♣ 7 5 4

R.R.
♠ A
♡ A 6 5
◇ 4 3 2
♣ A J 10 9 6 2

Having formed himself into a society for the prevention of cruelty to the Toucan, the Rabbit's bidding and play were reasonable enough. He had opened a somewhat unorthodox notrump to allow the Toucan every chance to sit back and watch the room go round, peacefully, as dummy. There was nothing wrong, either, with the final contract of 3 NT, which depended on a simple finesse. When, however, the Hog's king pounced on the ♣ Q, the Rueful Rabbit sat back, teeth clenched and eyes shut, to await the inevitable avalanche of spades. He was prepared for the worst, but somehow the inevitable didn't come to pass, and the first thing he beheld as he raised a doleful eyelid was not a spade but the ♡ J, beckoning to dummy's queen. Of course, she yielded, scoring the ninth, decisive trick for the Rabbit.

The Hog absolved himself unanimously of all blame, and as the flood of recriminations began to subside, he explained how and why his defence had been immaculate. Loath to suspect partner, even the Emeritus Professor, of wilful sabotage, he naturally assumed that the Rabbit had the king of spades behind the ace. On his play he was marked also with the ◇ K. Otherwise he would surely have finessed. The only hope of breaking the contract was, therefore, to find partner with ♡ A x x and to catch dummy's queen by leading the jack away from the king.

"The defence was too perfect to succeed," observed Colin the Corgi. "Everyone seems to have played superbly," agreed Oscar the Owl, who was still awake.

"Yes, didn't I?" exclaimed the Rabbit excitedly. "You know, there were times when I did just what H.H. would have done. I felt I *was* H.H., I was. . .er, not quite myself, perhaps. I. . ."

"He thinks he's me!" cried the Hideous Hog, deeply shocked. "Megalomania! Delusions of grandeur!"